Awakenings in America
and the Jesus People Movement

by Kent Allan Philpott

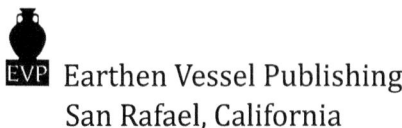

Earthen Vessel Publishing
San Rafael, California

*Awakenings in America
and the Jesus People Movement*

All rights reserved

Copyright © 2011 by Kent Allan Philpott

Published 2011 by
Earthen Vessel Publishing
San Rafael, CA 94903
www.earthenvessel.net

Interior Book Design and Layout by
www.integrativeink.com

ISBN: 978-0-9703296-4-6

No part of this publication may be reproduced,
stored in a retrieval system, or transmitted in any form or
by any means electronic, mechanical, photocopying,
recording, or otherwise, without the
written permission of the author or publisher.

Dedication

This book is dedicated to my twin daughters, Jenna Maree and Laura Elizabeth, students at the University of California at Santa Barbara.

Acknowledgements

Sincere appreciation and thanks to the following people:
Katie Leslie Coddaire Philpott who edited the book and generally encouraged and supported her husband.

David Hoyt who, as a living part of the fourth awakening, provided a first hand history.

Table of Contents

Foreword xiii

Preface xvii

Introduction 1

    A DESCRIPTION OF AWAKENING 2

    A BIBLICAL AWAKENING 3

    A SIGN AND WONDER 4

    WHAT HAPPENED AT THIS AWAKENING? 5

    NORMAL AND AWAKENING TIMES 5

    ONE WAY, JESUS CHRIST 6

    THE AMERICAN AWAKENINGS 7

    AWAKENINGS ARE NOT UNUSUAL 10

    AWAKENING HISTORIES ARE COMPLEX 10

One: The first awakening in America (a.1734 - a.1742) 13

    EVENTS PRECEDING THE AWAKENING 13

    SOLOMON STODDARD 14

    THEODORE FRELINGHUYSEN 16

    THE TENNENTS AND THE 'LOG COLLEGE' 18

    JONATHAN EDWARDS 19

    GEORGE WHITEFIELD—THE GREAT AWAKENER 22

THE BEGINNINGS OF EVANGELICALISM?	25
DARK SIDE OF THE FIRST AWAKENING	26
A GREATER NUMBER OF FAITHFUL CHRISTIANS	30
IMPACT OF THE GREAT AWAKENING	31
THE UNIQUENESS OF AWAKENINGS	33

Two: The second awakening in America (a.1798 - a.1835) 34

DATING THE AWAKENING	35
THE AGE OF REASON	37
ON THE EVE OF THE SECOND AWAKENING	38
THE AWAKENING IN THE WEST	39
STODDARD TO EDWARDS TO DWIGHT— THE AWAKENING IN THE EAST	42
ASAHEL NETTLETON	44
CHARLES FINNEY AND THE SECOND HALF OF THE SECOND AWAKENING	45
DARK SIDE OF THE SECOND AWAKENING	49
THE RISE OF ARMINIAN THEOLOGY AND THE DECLINE OF CALVINISTIC THEOLOGY	52
RISE OF AMERICAN BIBLE-BASED CULTS	55
IMPACT OF THE SECOND AWAKENING	57
CONCLUDING REMARKS	60

Three: The Third Awakening in America (a.1857 - a.1859) 61

DATES	61
DISTINGUISHING CHARACTERISTICS OF AWAKENINGS	62
BETWEEN THE SECOND AND THIRD AWAKENING	63
CANADIAN AWAKENINGS AND THE PALMERS	65

THE NOON BUSINESSMAN'S PRAYER MEETING 66

WIDESPREAD SUPPORT FOR THE AWAKENING 71

ORR'S CHARACTERISTICS OF THE AWAKENING 71

THE AWAKENING'S IMPACT ON JEWS 73

DARK SIDE OF THE AWAKENING 74

THE AWAKENING AND THE ABOLITION MOVEMENT 75

THE AWAKENING AND THE CIVIL WAR 75

Four: The Fourth Awakening in America? The Jesus People Movement (a.1967 - a.1972) 76

DATES FOR THE JESUS PEOPLE MOVEMENT (A. 1967-A.1972) 76

"MOVEMENT" 77

EARLIER MOVEMENTS 78

HOW IT ALL BEGAN FOR ME 80

WHAT WE EXPERIENCED 84

THE ANCHOR RESCUE MISSION 86

OUR FIRST CHRISTIAN HOUSES 87

MORE CHRISTIAN HOUSES 89

LONNIE FRISBEE AND CHUCK SMITH 90

DAVID "MO" BERG 90

A SECOND NOTABLE MIRACLE 91

A PARA-CHURCH MINISTRY 92

WORK CREWS 92

JOYFUL NOISE 93

PSYCHEDELIC CONVERSIONS? 96

ON THE ROAD 97

TOWARD THE CLOSE OF THE AWAKENING 99

THE DARK SIDE OF THE JESUS PEOPLE MOVEMENT 101

PROPHECY, SIGNS, WONDERS, AND HEALING 101

THE CHILDREN OF GOD 103

JIM JONES AND THE PEOPLE'S TEMPLE 105

THE SHEPHERDING MOVEMENT 107

ONE MORE THOUGHT ON THE DARK SIDE 108

THE BRIGHT SIDE OF THE JESUS PEOPLE MOVEMENT 109

THE JESUS PEOPLE MOVEMENT—A FOURTH GREAT AWAKENING? .. 111

MURRAY'S MARKS 112

BEARDSLEY'S MARKS 116

EDWARDS' MARKS 119

CONCLUSION 120

Five: The last awakening (?-?) 122

WILL AMERICA EXPERIENCE ANOTHER AWAKENING? 122

NORMAL AND AWAKENING TIMES 123

AWAKENINGS ARE GOING ON SOMEWHERE MOST OF THE TIME 123

THE LAST GREAT AWAKENING 124

ISRAEL AND THE LAST GREAT AWAKENING 125

JESUS POINTS TO A FUTURE SAVING EVENT FOR JERUSALEM 126

ALL ISRAEL WILL BE SAVED 128

DO WE HAVE A PART? 129

Appendix A: A summary of Jonathan Edwards' Distinguishing marks of the work of the Spirit of God 130

AUTHOR'S INTRODUCTION 130

SUMMARY OR BRIEF OUTLINE OF DISTINGUISHING MARKS OF A WORK OF THE SPIRIT OF GOD 132

EDWARD'S UNTITLED INTRODUCTION 132

- SECTION A 133
- SECTION B 148
- SECTION C 155

Appendix B: Discussion and summary of Jonathan Edwards' The Religious Affections 165

- EDWARDS' INTRODUCTION: 165
- A COMMENTARY ON THE INTRODUCTION 172
- SUMMARY OF EDWARDS' BOOK, *THE RELIGIOUS AFFECTIONS* 176
- "NOT CERTAIN SIGNS" 176
- DISTINGUISHING SIGNS 178

Appendix C: Movements that preceded and followed the Jesus People Movement 180

- ONE—THAT WHICH PRECEDED 180
- THE WESLEYAN HOLINESS MOVEMENT 180
- THE AZUSA STREET REVIVAL 181
- THE HEALING REVIVAL OF THE 1950s 181
- THE CATHOLIC RENEWAL AND CHARISMATIC MOVEMENTS 182
- IMPACT OF PENTECOSTAL UNDERSTANDINGS ON EVANGELISM 183
- A SHARP CONTRAST 184
- TWO—THAT WHICH FOLLOWED 185
- THE VINEYARD AND JOHN WIMBER (THIRD WAVE) 185
- THE TORONTO BLESSING 187
- THE "FOURTH WAVE"? 188
- AN EXPLANATION 189
- THERE IS YET ANOTHER VIEW 189

Index 191

Foreword

The mysterious events and seemingly inexplicable timing of the "awakenings" of the Christian religion have captivated laymen, clergy, theologians, and historians for nearly three centuries now. The sudden appearance of these great revivals, their just-as-sudden disappearance, and the changed ecclesiastical, moral, social, political, and cultural landscapes that remained in their aftermath have made them one of the most meaningful—and controversial—topics in the history of the American Church. Lingering behind these historical and theological discussions are an enduring set of questions: What qualifies as an awakening? What role, if any, does human agency play in their promotion and duration? When and where might one happen again?

Kent Philpott comes to this topic not merely as an academic interpreter but as someone who was a key player in the beginnings of the Jesus People movement of the late 1960s and early 1970s—a revival among American youth which may well have been the largest religious awakening to take place in the 20th-century. Between the years of 1967 and (depending on one's locale) sometime in the mid-1970s, literally hundreds of thousands of American youth—from hardcore hippies to rock music-friendly church kids—joined in a seemingly spontaneous outpouring known as the "Jesus movement." Street evangelism, communal "Jesus houses," Christian coffeehouses, Jesus-testifying rock bands, and "One Way" bumper stickers became a ubiquitous fact of life all across North America. Kent Philpott was there at its inception. A young Air Force veteran from Southern California who had enrolled at the Southern Baptists' Golden Gate Seminary, Philpott walked the streets of Haight-Ashbury evangelizing practically anyone he encountered during the 1967 "Summer of Love." Later, as part of the Evangelical Concerns group he became a leader of a string of communal houses and evangelistic ministries in the Bay Area and eventually went to England to help evangelize the youth culture there.

Coming of age as a seminary student, pastor, and evangelist in the midst of the "Jesus Revolution," Philpott was surrounded by a flood of incredible life-changing conversions, enthusiastic worship, earnest discipleship, and—yes, even—perceived signs and wonders. In the midst of those heady circumstances he came to think of revival as the natural, default position in the Christian experience. And then—suddenly—it all seemed to stop.

In the more than thirty years that have passed since it became clear that the day of the Jesus People was over, Kent Philpott has become aware that as a participant in that awakening he was swept up in something rare, something beyond his control, and something beyond his ready understanding. Nonetheless, he has not been able to shake the powerful influence those days had upon his life and the lives of an entire generation—he cannot help but try to come to grips with exactly what happened back then on the streets of Haight-Ashbury. In the process, he has undertaken a thorough study of the earlier great revivals in American history, read the writings of both the awakenings' proponents and enemies, and studied the accounts and analysis of those who later wrote about them. As a pastor and a student of the Bible, Philpott has attempted to grapple with the biblical and theological arguments that have informed these debates. His honesty and sincerity in this quest are borne out by the reality that his concepts and judgments on the matter of awakenings and revivals (even the one in which he was personally involved) have not remained static: his understanding has evolved and some important, once dearly-held, opinions have changed over the years.

Certainly as a memoir and analysis of the Jesus People movement, this book will become an important part of what is becoming an ever-growing body of literature. Beyond that, however, is its usefulness as a source on the broader biblical, theological, and historical questions surrounding the enigma that are the "great awakenings." Whether your interest is primarily historical or theological, whether it results from an interest in American religion or whether you are simply concerned as a believer about the role and need for revival, Kent Philpott's *The Great American Awakenings and the Jesus People Movement* will serve as an important perspective on the place of revivals and awakenings within the Church, as well as within the larger American religious and cultural landscape.

> Larry Eskridge
> Wheaton, IL
> August 18, 2009

Preface

In 1996, I began an independent study of the "great" awakenings in America. As a seminary student in the 1960s, I became aware of these revivals of religion, as they were often called, but some three decades later I recalled next to nothing about them. Reading again about Jonathan Edwards, Gilbert Tennent, George Whitefield, Jonathan Dickinson, Samuel Davies, Samuel Blair, and many others, I thrilled to the accounts of the extraordinary power of a sovereign God. And then my life changed as a result of what I found while reading about the second awakening of 1798-1835.

A famous debate between Asahel Nettleton and Charles Finney occurred during the middle of that second awakening which focused on the "old measures" championed by Nettleton and the "new measures" championed by Finney. As I studied it, my theology of conversion was severely shaken. The story of that journey is recounted in *Are You Really Born Again?*, published by Evangelical Press in 1998, with a revised edition in 2005. The awakenings themselves, along with what happened during those times of outpourings of God's Holy Spirit, have forever been impressed on my mind.

In my preaching ministry I have loved retelling the stories of the awakenings, and during the close of 2007, I set about to do it again for the congregation of the Miller Avenue Baptist Church of Mill Valley, CA. They heard six sermons sandwiched around a sermon by my old friend David Hoyt, who was one of the leaders of the Jesus People Movement. The glory of God in his saving, sovereign work in David's life and the changed lives of countless others once more thrilled the hearers. It is my hope that many will give glory and honor to our great God when this book is read.

During David Hoyt's visit, we took advantage of the situation, both by having David preach and by discussing together what we recalled about the Jesus People Movement, recording it in DVD format. We captured two hours of material, which can be obtained at www.earthenvessel.net.

My intent was to make this as short a book as possible. Many good books on the awakenings have been published over the years, many in great detail, so my approach here is to use a *broad brush* and concentrate on the main events and the larger lessons, both good and bad.

One of my goals is to show that the Jesus People Movement, from now on referred to as either the JPM or the fourth awakening, qualifies as an awakening alongside the first three. I hope to prove this or at least to make a good case for it.

Another goal is to focus on the "dark side" or excesses of awakenings. Each of the awakenings was troubled to some degree. I will critically examine some of these more negative elements, so that we might have a more complete view of the awakenings, with a resulting hope of avoiding these, should another awakening come along.

The dark sides of awakenings threaten to tarnish them or relegate them to something other than miraculous works of the Holy Spirit; they add up to nothing more than humanly engineered revivalism. For some, the trouble with awakenings is that they are indeed outpourings of God's Spirit. If they are miraculous, then deists and atheists, both theoretical and practical, have to re-evaluate their entire philosophical world view. In much the same way, atheists and deists must deny the virgin birth as well as other miracles, since what follows the admission of the reality of a virgin birth is too much for them to accept. My point is that the awakenings, including the JPM, had their human, perhaps even demonic elements, yet the hand of God was over and above the darkness and distortion, regardless of the source, human or demonic.

There is something more. The final chapter goes beyond the original plan for the book but seemed, nevertheless, to fit in a way I could not ignore. Let me explain.

At the time of the sermons on the awakenings, October and November of 2007, I was also teaching through chapters 9, 10, and 11 of Paul's letter to the Romans for our church's Tuesday night Bible study. Once again, I was challenged by verses 11-12 and verses 25-26 of chapter 11. As someone who embraces a Reformed theology, I was prepared to interpret the passages along customary replacement theology lines. By "replacement theology" I mean the concept that the Church replaces the nation Israel and that whatever was promised to Israel finds fulfillment in the Church. But I was stopped short this time. The commentators I had been consulting for the Bible study—James M. Boice, F.F. Bruce, Matthew Henry, Charles Hodge, and others—plainly spoke of something other than what is normally part of a replacement theology. They suggested that there would be another awakening, which would in fact be the last and greatest awakening of all time, when "all Israel" would be saved. Persuaded by what I now understand, I am departing from one of the doctrines of the original sixteenth century reformers, mainly Martin Luther. Oh yes, I am still fully amongst those who love the Doctrines of Grace, but on this one point I have another view.

After Paul declares that the salvation of Israel will occur after the "fullness of the Gentiles" has been accomplished, he launches into one of the most beautiful doxologies in Scripture.

> Oh, the depth of the riches and wisdom and knowledge of God! How unsearchable are his judgments and how inscrutable his ways!

> "For who has known the mind of the Lord, or
> who has been his counselor? Or who has given
> a gift to him that he might be repaid?"
> For from him and through him and to him
> are all things. To him be glory forever. Amen
> (Romans 11:33-36, ESV)

Iain H. Murray's *Revival and Revivalism* (The Banner of Truth Trust, 1994), Thomas S. Kidd's *The Great Awakening* (Yale University Press, 2007), and J. Edwin Orr's *The Event of the Century: the 1857-1858 Awakening* (International Awakening Press, Wheaton, IL, 1989) figured very prominently in the preparation of this book. Theirs are scholarly and meticulous histories, unlike this brief treatment. I am also indebted to *Christian History* magazine, particularly Volume VIII, No. 3 Issue 23.

Not a historian, my intent has been to show the basic nature of awakenings so that others may appreciate and understand them as they experience them, with a view to avoiding the dark sides and to grasping the essential and fundamental purpose of awakenings—to revive God's people and sweep new believers into His Church. If only I had read this kind of book in 1967!

No bibliography is provided with this book; rather I direct further research to the title index in Iain H. Murray's *Revival and Revivalism*, to the bibliography in Larry Eskridge's *God's Forever Family: The Jesus People Movement in America,* and to the bibliography of J. Edwin Orr's *The Event of the Century.*

Introduction

There have been many awakenings[1] over the centuries—some large enough to be called "People Movements" and some very small, with variations in between. Individual churches, small towns, regions, states, and nations have experienced awakenings. It may have been that a single family or even a lone individual has experienced an outpouring of God's Spirit. This is based on what I have read over the years.

What is an awakening? It would be presumptuous on my part to claim to authoritatively answer the question; I can only give my impressions of what an awakening is, based on experience and research. Some awakenings seem to come suddenly, while others appear to have taken their time to build up momentum. The First Great Awakening may have begun a generation or more before the ministry of Jonathan Edwards during the 1730s, moving from village to village—a little here, a little there—and all under the pastoral ministry of Solomon Stoddard, Edwards' grandfather. Then, in 1735 at Northampton, Massachusetts, events began to unfold that eventually earned the designation of America's first awakening. Awakenings brought life, strength, and health. However, mixed up in it all were those conditions called the "dark sides" of revival; the aftermath of an awakening was not all glory. Some of the most bizarre organizations, movements, and

---

1 The terms "awakening" and "revival" are generally used interchangeably, and I follow this same pattern. "Outpouring" or being "wrought upon" have also been used by Jonathan Edwards and others to designate an awakening or revival.

theologies have been spawned during times of awakening. Nothing is neat and clean when it comes to awakenings.

A description of awakening

That which is genuine and authentic about an awakening or revival is something God does, though God is not in all of it. This is contrary to much of my early thinking and experience. At the church where my conversion took place and at the first church of which I was pastor, we routinely held both a fall and spring revival. These were preaching events that were well planned out and organized. Certainly, the motive was good—we wanted to see people believe in our Lord Jesus Christ. We put into place the standard processes such as advertising, mailers, visitation of unbelievers in the community, and other means, in order to promote the revival. These usually proved to be successful, based on seeing some "decisions" made at the altar call or invitation. My current view is that, though we plan, pray, and preach for revival, God will act according to his good pleasure and purpose as to when, how, and where his Spirit will be powerfully engaged to call unbelievers to a saving faith in Jesus Christ. My point is that genuine awakenings are of God entirely and are not the result of human effort (as though we could tell God how to do his work).

Good, however, can come from planned and humanly engineered "revivals." Struggling Christians may be encouraged to walk more closely with their Lord, unbelievers may begin to live more ethically, and there may be some genuine conversions to Christ, with people being baptized and joining churches. I have seen plenty of these personally, but an awakening is altogether another thing. No real planning necessarily precedes or causes a sovereign outpouring of the Spirit—perhaps some praying for and desiring for revival goes on behind the scenes, and it is almost always the case that some of God's people are praying for revival—but an awakening is of another sort, and I hope to show this by describing the great American awakenings.

Have awakenings come as a direct result of the prayers of God's people? The prayers of earnest Christians seem to have an effect, yet I cannot be sure. Before each of the American awakenings, people were praying. Generations of Christians have prayed for awakening to come, and in some of those generations, many did not live to see an answer to their prayers, while others did. This is not easily understood, but when an awakening did come, it was a result of God's sovereign will. God was not manipulated into bringing awakening. We are Christians and not magicians, and we do not tell God what or how to do his work. Once we think we can get God to act, even on the basis of our praying, we have crossed the line into magical thinking. We can and will pray, plan, and preach for revival, but God alone brings it.

A biblical awakening

The Church in Jerusalem experienced an awakening and thousands were converted. (There were events in the Old Testament that may also be referred to as awakenings.)

Just moments before his ascension—Jesus' return to the Father in heaven—he directed his disciples to remain in Jerusalem and "wait for the promise of the Father" (Acts 1:4). He said, "John baptized with water, but you will be baptized with the Holy Spirit not many days from now" (Acts 1:5).

The promise of the baptism with the Holy Spirit was to empower the apostles to be Jesus' witnesses. "But you will receive power when the Holy Spirit has come upon you, and you will be my witnesses in Jerusalem, and in all Judea and Samaria, and to the end of the earth" (Acts 1:8). When the empowering came on what we call the Day of Pentecost, Peter preached a sermon, and about three thousand people were converted.

The young, growing church in Jerusalem immediately "devoted themselves to the apostles' teaching and fellowship, to the breaking of bread and the prayers" (Acts 2:42). These areas of devotion of the early believers are characteristic also in times of awakening. The Pentecostal converts wanted to hear the words of the apostles, they valued the spiritual community, they prayed, and they celebrated the Lord's Supper. In addition, "many wonders and signs were being done through the apostles" (Acts 2:43).

A sign and wonder

One of the "wonders and signs" served to dramatically expand that first Pentecostal awakening. On their way to the temple for the morning prayers, Peter and John encountered a man lame from birth. This man was asking for alms, and the apostles had no money to give him, but Peter commanded him, "In the name of Jesus Christ of Nazareth, rise up and walk" (Acts 3:6). And he did rise up; in fact, he was walking, even leaping, and he was praising God.

The lame man was well known, and his healing came to the attention of the religious leaders. Such a sign or miracle troubled them, since it was done "in the name of Jesus Christ of Nazareth."[2] Peter and John were called before the great council of the leaders of Israel to ascertain the facts. The apostles affirmed that Jesus was responsible for the healing, the same Jesus whom the council had brought to trial before Pilate. But now he was alive, raised from the dead. More than that, they declared the great truth that characterizes all true awakenings, both then and now, that "there is salvation in no one else, for there is no other name under heaven given among men by which we must be saved" (Acts 4:12). The council dismissed Peter and John but charged them "not to speak or teach at all in the name of Jesus" (Acts 4:18).

Upon their release the two apostles sought out some members of the church (numbers had reached over five thou-

---

2 "In the name of Jesus" means because of and through the person of Jesus Christ. It is not a magical phrase that once uttered is powerful in and of itself.

sand believers already) and gave a report of the events that had just taken place. Immediately, the church prayed to the "Sovereign Lord," and near the end of the prayer asked that God "grant to your servants to continue to speak your word with all boldness, while you stretch out your hand to heal, and signs and wonders are performed through the name of your holy servant Jesus" (Acts 4:29-30). After that prayer the place where they were meeting "was shaken, and they were all filled with the Holy Spirit and continued to speak the word of God with boldness" (Acts 4:31).

What happened at this awakening?

The following describes the core events of the awakening(s) in Jerusalem:

The apostles waited for the baptizing of the Holy Spirit to give them power to witness for and about Jesus. It is easy to imagine that the apostles might be fearful, considering what had happened to Jesus himself. They were away from home and had suffered a defection (Judas), but they obeyed Jesus. Then the empowering came on the very Day of Pentecost, and Peter preached, and three thousand were converted. This baptism was far different from the baptism of John—now God's Spirit was poured out. People were convicted of their sin, whole heartedly turned to their Messiah Jesus, and were even baptized "in his name."

After the Pentecost events, there were more signs and wonders, and despite the threats and warnings aimed at them, the apostles had boldness to continue to speak out about Jesus, which resulted in more people being converted.

Normal and awakening times

"Signs and wonders"—miracles that pointed to the messiahship and Lordship of Jesus Christ—are clearly present in the biblical accounts of the life of Jesus and in the life of the early Church. Many theologians in the Reformed tradition say that signs and wonders ceased once the Holy Spirit was given to the Church and the New Testament was published. I will say here that I agree with this doctrine but only partially. In "normal times" there are few, if any, signs and wonders observed or experienced, but in "awakening times" signs and wonders will be observed, even in abundance, or they may be absent all together. Signs and wonders are not necessary to designate something as an awakening, but they may appear.

The Jerusalem awakening was not a "normal" event; it was special and accomplished by the Sovereign God. Life generally returned to normal after the Samarian (Acts 8), Caesarean (Acts10), and Ephesian (Acts 19) awakenings. From Acts 20 on to the end of Luke's account, it appears that "normal" times had come to the Church. This is what we find in accounts of the American awakenings as well. There are times when the Holy Spirit is poured out and many are converted, accompanied by signs and wonders. However, most times must be considered as normal, when considerably fewer experience conversion and there is little evidence of signs and wonders.

One way, Jesus Christ

A bold proclamation of a crucified and risen Savior was a hallmark of the apostolic awakening preaching. This is true down through the ages. Churches that preach an untarnished gospel experience growth[3], while others whose message is something other or less than a clear bold gospel participate to a much lesser degree—perhaps not at all. During normal times, bold preaching of the gospel may not yield large success, though there will be some, if the preachers are patient. This was true for me during the JPM. My preaching efforts, poor as they were, were blessed, sometimes extremely so. Many times I witnessed people, quite new to the Faith and without

---

3 "Growth may not always be numerical; in fact, numerical *loss* may more accurately reflect actual spiritual growth. Numerical growth may be a misleading indicator of the Holy Spirit's involvement, as the recent growth in "mega-churches" due to a focus on entertainment and meeting "felt needs" has demonstrated.

any real training, see many converts through a simple testimony or halting sermon. Then after the awakening subsided, my preaching and that of others did not see the same results.

Acts 4:12, a statement that there is salvation in only Jesus, characterized the Jerusalem awakening. What is true in all the awakenings is that the exclusive claims of Jesus Christ are highly visible. The essentials of the gospel are preached, including doctrines that typically offend unbelievers: sin, death, hell, judgment, cross, grave, empty tomb, resurrection, ascension, and second coming—these are fully disclosed without equivocation.

Questions that may be asked, though without anticipation of concise and clear answers, are, How does the baptism of the Holy Spirit that Jesus spoke of in Acts 1:4-8 work? Who or what is baptized? Is it the preacher, the hearers, or even the message that is baptized or empowered by the Holy Spirit? Is it one of these, or two, or maybe all three? My response is that it is somewhat of a moot point, since we really do not need to know. All we need to know is that awakenings are the work of the Holy Spirit of God. If pressed or tempted to pick one of the three, I would say that the message is empowered by the Holy Spirit, and then the hearer is brought face to face with his or her need of a Savior.

It is vital to see the difference between normal and awakening times. Without understanding the difference, there is a much greater chance that there will be distortions and aberrations, those aspects of awakenings that may be called "wild fire" or the "dark side." As the accounts of the American awakenings are described, this subject will be a particular focus of this book.

The American Awakenings

Three American awakenings have been generally recognized. The first, from roughly 1734 to 1742; the second, from 1798 to 1835 (this one had two rather distinct parts); and the third, from 1857 to 1858. I am proposing that the JPM should be considered a fourth awakening. There have been perhaps hundreds or thousands of other revivals or awakenings, both in America and around the world, but small enough not to come to the attention of a society as a whole. Individual churches, groupings of churches, small towns, and so on—these have experienced outpourings of God's Spirit in the same manner as the larger awakenings. I am aware of this simply because of my research and because of what I have come to know and experience.

Awakenings are so designated because they meet certain criteria, marks, or characteristics that distinguish them from ordinary events occurring during normal times. We will examine the JPM in particular, using three lists of criteria, one from Jonathan Edwards, a second from Frank Beardsley, an American Baptist writing at the beginning of the twentieth century, and a third from Iain Murray. Murray, a recognized expert on awakenings and revivals, provides, in my view, the most important list to help determine if an event is indeed an awakening.

In Jonathan Edwards' *A Narrative of the Surprising Work of God in Northampton, Mass, 1735,* it is possible to detect the main elements in the spiritual awakening that came to his congregation: (1) There had been similar events under the ministry of Edwards' grandfather Solomon Stoddard; (2) There was a definite time when the awakening began; (3) People earnestly discussed eternal things; (4) There developed awareness of sin and the fear of judgment; (5) There arose a concern for salvation; (6) Christian people were renewed; (7) Those converted were vitally interested in prayer and Bible study; (8) Church attendance increased; and (9) There was a gradual withdrawing of the Spirit.

C.C. Caen, editor of *The Great Awakening*, lists Edwards' "five luminous signs that a revival is of God": (1) It raises people's esteem of Jesus as Son of God and Savior of the world; (2) It leads them to turn away from sin and toward holiness;

(3) It increases their love for the Bible; (4) It grounds them in the basic biblical truth; and (5) It works greater love for and service to God and other people.[4]

Frank Beardsley, in *A History of American Revivals*, lists the following marks of the revival in writing of the first great awakening (my paraphrases): (1) There was an interest in eternal things; (2) Conversations centered on theological themes; (3) The world began to hold less interest; (4) People pressed into the kingdom of God; (5) Many conversions now followed; (6) This same pattern spread to surrounding towns; and (7) The revival or awakening sprang up independently in various areas.[5]

Iain H. Murray, in *Revival and Revivalism*, lists marks of the 1858 awakening that are common to any true spiritual awakening. Murray's list is as follows: (1) Hunger for the Word of God, for prayer, and for serious Christian literature; (2) A sense of wonder and profound seriousness; (3) The same work evident in many places at once; (4) Joyful praise and readiness to witness; (5) New energy in practical Christian service; (6) The recovery of family worship and family religion; and (7) An observable raising of the whole moral tone of society.[6]

The first three American awakenings fulfilled these criteria, and I will attempt to show that the JPM does as well.

My own list of criteria for what constitutes an awakening is based on the above and my own research: (1) A beginning point occurs, however indefinite, when there is a direct and bold witness of the historical and biblically orthodox gospel to unbelievers with numbers of conversions taking place; (2) Some unbelievers are angered, reject the gospel, and may seek to thwart the efforts of Christian preachers; (3) Those

---

[4] C. C. Caen, ed., *The Great Awakening* (New haven, CT: The Yale University Press, 1972), 228-248.
[5] Frank Beardsley, *A History of American Revivals* (American Tract Society: Boston, 1904), various.
[6] Iain H. Murray, *Revival and Revivalism* (Carlisle, PA: The Banner of Truth Trust, 1994), 348.

who are converted become aware of their sin and have an unusual interest in Jesus; (4) The new converts have an intense interest in the Bible and will want to "devour" it; (5) New converts will want to be baptized and desire to witness to family and friends; (6) They will have a love for prayer; (7) They will display a turning away from sin, often dramatically discarding objects used in sinful behavior, such as drugs and drug paraphernalia; (8) They will begin to become responsible citizens; (9) They will show an interest in helping others who are needy; (10) There comes a slow and gradual ending to the awakening in general, though it may seem to linger for some months or years; (11) Distortions of and imitations of the awakening begin to appear; and (12) Over a period of time, perhaps several decades, those who were truly converted in the awakening will continue following Jesus, despite stumbling, while others who were merely attracted to the awakening because of the fun and excitement will fall away over time and will not identify with Jesus at all.

Awakenings are not unusual

Awakenings are going on today, in many places all at once, without the participants in one area necessarily aware of an outpouring in another. But these are miniature versions of the larger awakenings. Awakenings of whatever size and duration have a beginning point that is often indefinite, and they will have an end point that may also be indefinite. For instance, my reckoning is that the JPM ended in the San Francisco Bay Area in late 1972. Others say 1975 or even 1978. The JPM did not arrive in Los Angeles, according to my recollection, until 1968 and lasted until about 1975. In Atlanta, Georgia, the JPM arrived about 1969 and lasted until about 1975.

Awakening histories are complex

Thomas S. Kidd's *The Great Awakening* illustrates the fact that awakenings are difficult to chronicle. Kidd's excellent work describes dozens of preachers, pastors, churches, times, and places associated with America's first awakening. Many accounts of awakenings name only the principle preachers and a few other highlights. The JPM is so very complex, that I approach writing of it with some trepidation. Though I was engaged in it, still I only saw a small piece of it; indeed, exhaustive histories may not even be possible for a generation or two from now. However, I will attempt to use a broad brush while writing of my own impressions and experiences only.

Now we will look at the first three American awakenings, noting only the highlights of each, and then we will take a closer and personal look at the JPM. Finally, we will consider the possibility of one last very great awakening.

One:
The first awakening in America
(a.1734 - a.1742)

The first awakening in America is often termed "The Great Awakening" because of its large impact on a rather small population—about one million people inhabited the American colonies at that time. The years usually designated as the beginning and ending points of the awakening are only approximate. Beginnings and endings of awakenings are often difficult to pin-point. It seems that for some years preceding 1734 and for some years following 1742 there were individual churches and clusters of churches in specific locations that experienced an outpouring of the Spirit. However, those who have studied the period combined with those who lived it, generally confine the largest part of the awakening to the years given above.

Events preceding the awakening

It is often thought that dire times precede awakenings and lead to or precipitate them. The reverse of that theory, then, would be that good and prosperous times do not precede awakenings. However, the conditions of a people, whether good or ill, probably have little or nothing to do with awakenings. None of this can be conclusively verified or rejected. In every age there are signs of strength and weakness at once. Historians have generally reported that the first awakening was preceded by a slumping economy, moral decline, religious indifference, and political turmoil. The colonial Americans were therefore, it is thought, ready for revival.

Colonial America of the eighteenth century indeed showed worrying signs of decay. The strong faith that had brought the early settlers to America, many of whom had been anxious for religious freedom and toleration, had been diluted. The grandchildren and great grandchildren of the immigrants had drifted from the vibrant faith of their forbearers. However, history does not attest to the presence of a decadent, immoral, and crazed people. There were great churches and outstanding preachers, and though there were also great sinners, as there always are, the culture as a whole seemed generally healthy.

Could it be that some want to see awakenings as mere products of the constant process of psycho-sociology, whereby natural selection takes place within a human population, and conditions occur to separate out that which is harmful? If that were the case, then no awakening would actually be a work of the Spirit of God. Any culture could be characterized as being in decline at any given point. There are elements of a population that are prospering and elements that are not—this is all business as usual. My view is that the awakenings considered in this book were from the hand and will of God and not the primary result of other factors.

Solomon Stoddard

As previously stated, the dates for the first awakening are an estimate only. The beginning of the first American awakening may date back to the ministry of Solomon Stoddard. While pastor of the First (Congregational) Church of Northampton, Massachusetts, he experienced what he called "harvests" in 1679, 1683, 1696, 1712, and 1718. Awakenings were also reported in Hartford and Windom, Connecticut, as well as in Taunton, Massachusetts. These events were confined to local churches for a brief period of time and involved a small group of people. It seems probable that these movements of the Spirit were but a prelude to what was to come and not part of the actual awakening that commenced in 1734.

Solomon Stoddard was a pastor who desired revival and prayed and preached for one. He argued that a revival was desperately needed but saw little success. Stoddard knew that revival depended upon biblical preaching that emphasized the gospel of Christ. He promoted preaching about "the danger of damnation" and warned against only preaching about moral duty and other more pleasant topics current to the day. He knew that ministers must fearlessly awaken people to their desperate condition and preach, not to entertain or impress with fine words and fit phrases, but to clearly warn of the consequences of sin. This was the heart of Solomon Stoddard.

Stoddard identified three results of revival or, as he called it, an "outpouring of the Spirit of God": One, saints are quickened. Believers, having become spiritually deadened are stirred once again to prayer, worship, holiness, and brotherly love. Two, sinners are converted. The preaching of the gospel has unusually powerful effects on the unconverted, and they are brought to a saving faith in Christ. Three, many who are not converted do become more religious. This last point may seem unusual, but it is also what I observed in the JPM. Not everyone who is attracted to the gospel is converted, at least not right away, but they may nevertheless go through personal reformation.

Stoddard also understood that the church needed to be revived from time to time, that revival was not a constant experience, because people will eventually drift into spiritual deadness. So profound was his passion for revival that he backed what became known as the "half-way covenant," which had its beginning in 1662. By that period in Colonial history, it was obvious to the majority of the clergy that religion had reached an unhappy state compared to what it had been for those who had left the homeland to come to the new world. This concern was genuine.

The original goal of the half-way covenant was to increase church membership and reach out to large numbers who had no part in Christianity. Under the covenant, people were admitted to church membership without requiring evidence of conversion. It was thought that if people would partake of the sacraments—baptism and the Lord's Supper—these would become saving events, "converting ordinances" in and of themselves, and thus the churches would grow. Eventually, this practice went so far as to allow persons into the pastoral ministry itself without requiring them to show or admit Christian conversion. One could become a doctor, lawyer, merchant, or minister, all on the basis of choice and not divine calling. After a period of time, the churches were full of people, however sincere and outwardly godly, who were not converted and whose ministers were sometimes not converted either. This is a phenomenon that has repeated itself throughout our entire Christian history.

Solomon Stoddard's grandson, Jonathan Edwards, became associate pastor of the First Church of Northampton in 1727 and took over the senior pastorate of that church two years later, following the death of his grandfather. What the new pastor discovered was that he had inherited a church filled with non-Christians. This revelation led to the preaching which would help usher in America's first awakening.

Theodore Frelinghuysen

Solomon Stoddard ministered in the New England colonies, mainly Massachusetts; but in the middle colonies, especially New Jersey, it was Theodore Jacob Frelinghuysen who made a considerable impact for the gospel of Christ. Born in Germany, educated in Holland, he came to New York in 1719 and later settled in New Jersey's Raritan Valley to pastor churches founded by Dutch immigrants. He had been influenced by the

Pietism movement that had emerged among Lutherans. The Pietists were concerned about heart religion and holy living; indeed, Pietism was a revival movement among Lutheran people in particular.

To Frelinghuysen's dismay, he found the churches for which he was responsible to be in much the same condition as the church Edwards would later pastor—filled with people who were not genuinely converted to Christ. He found a religious, church-going people, but who apparently had not actually been born again by the Spirit of God. In the face of this circumstance, he declared that only those who were truly converted could hope to have salvation. Of course, he was continuously attacked by other ministers who had differing opinions.

Deeply influenced by Pietism, Frelinghuysen preached conversion and holy living. Slowly, his ministry began to see results. He, like Stoddard, was a forerunner of what would come later; indeed, his tireless evangelistic efforts and gospel preaching at minimum paved the way for the larger awakening.

George Whitefield, who became the most important preacher of the first awakening, had the opportunity to meet both Edwards and Frelinghuysen during the early 1740s. Of Frelinghuysen, Whitefield said,

> Among those who came to hear the Word, were several ministers, whom the Lord has been pleased to honour, in making them instruments of bringing many sons to glory. One was a Dutch Calvinistic minister, named Freeling Housen, pastor of a congregation about four miles from New Brunswick. He is a worthy old soldier of Jesus Christ, and was the beginner of the great work which I trust the Lord is carrying on in these parts.[7]

---

[7] "Theodore Jacob Frelinghuysen in the Middle Colonies," A. K. Curtis, A. V. Laughner and K. J. Hardman, eds., *Christian History Magazine*, Vol. VIII, No. 3, Issue 23, 1989, 11.

The Tennents and the 'Log College'

Another major influence in the middle colonies came from the Tennent family. William Tennent, Sr., an Anglican priest, emigrated from Ireland in 1716 and later joined with the Presbyterians. He established a training school at Neshaminy, Pennsylvania for his four sons, three of whom were Gilbert, John, and William, Jr. In addition, Samuel Blair, Samuel Finley, William Robinson, and John Rowland were also students at the "Log College," and these all would become greatly used in the Great Awakening. In total, twenty men who trained at the college, which became the forerunner to Princeton University, would be involved in the work. The Log College of William Tennent became the symbol of what would be known as the "New Lights" as opposed to the "Old Lights." (Not to be confused with the New Measures and the Old Measures of the second awakening.) The New Lights included the Tennents, Frelinghuysen, Edwards, Whitefield, and all those who championed the awakening. Gilbert Tennent later worked alongside George Whitefield and figured large in the events of those days.

Gilbert Tennent, after his ordination in 1727 as a Presbyterian, began to pastor a church in New Brunswick, close to where Frelinghuysen pastored. Though of different denominations, the two pastors shared a common theology and concern for revival. It was Frelinghuysen who broke with certain denominational tendencies and began to have fellowship with other Christians despite differences in tradition. Gilbert Tennent then had an opportunity to study the ministry of Frelinghuysen and put some of what he valued into practice, especially Frelinghuysen's views on evangelism and gospel preaching.

It was the gospel labor and prayers of Solomon Stoddard, Theodore Frelinghuysen, the Tennents, Thomas Hooker in Hartford, Connecticut, and many others whose names are lost to history, that preceded the first awakening in America.

However, it is with Jonathan Edwards that most historians date the actual onset of that awakening.

Jonathan Edwards

Jonathan Edwards was born in 1703 in East Windsor, Connecticut, to a family steeped in Puritan traditions. His father Timothy Edwards was a pastor, and his mother Esther was a daughter of Solomon Stoddard. Eleven children were born to Timothy and Esther, Jonathan being the only boy.

Jonathan may be described as a child prodigy. He was learning Latin at the age of six, writing on complex and abstract points of theology at ten, and attending Yale University at age twelve or thirteen. After graduation in 1720, at the age of seventeen, he pastored the English Presbyterian Church in New York, but for only eight months. He then returned home and studied theology until 1724, when he was employed by his alma mater, Yale, as a tutor. In 1727 he served as an assistant to his grandfather Stoddard at the Congregational Church in Northampton, which by this time was the most influential church outside of Boston, and became pastor of the church in 1729, upon the death of his grandfather. It was then that Edwards became more keenly aware of the spiritual condition of the members of his congregation and resolved to do something about it.

God is sovereign in his work, this much is clear. That God chooses to work through earthen vessels is plain throughout the pages of Scripture. It is always so and was so in 1734, the year Edwards' preaching began to have an evangelistic purpose. He preached a series of sermons on justification by faith in the tried and proven way of the Puritans before him. His theology was Calvinistic through and through. Edwards considered it his work to proclaim the truth of Scripture and then depend on a sovereign God to do what only he could do.

I use 1734 and not 1735, as many historians designate, and the point is a minor one, but it was in December of 1734 that Edwards began to see favorable results from his preaching. For a period of six months, extending into 1735, some 300 people were converted, most of whom were members, as far as I can ascertain, of Edwards' church. This work of grace was not long confined to Northampton but soon spread to churches nearby. Some claimed that it was all due to an unusual enthusiasm that spread from community to community and not the work of the Spirit of God.

That the awakening spread may have been due, in some degree, to Edwards' writing of the events in Northampton. As the awakening began to decline in the area in which Edwards ministered, he wrote perhaps one of the most important books ever to be written in America, *A Narrative of the Surprising Work of God, in Northampton, Mass., 1735.*[8]

Some twenty townships in Western Massachusetts and Connecticut experienced awakening of some intensity as a result of the "*Narrative.*" Also, as word spread of the events in Northampton, people who wanted a first-hand account took away with them what they had seen. And what they had seen and heard were people confessing Christ as Savior and Lord through the mere agency of the preaching of a clear gospel message of salvation.

The *Narrative* went through some twenty printings and found its way to London where John Wesley read it and passed it on to his friend George Whitefield. John Wesley's own preaching was encouraged by the book, and he began to see evidence around him of awakening as well. Whitefield read the book and decided to come to America to see for himself the surprising work of God; and this event, the first of seven of Whitefield's journeys to America starting in 1739, marks the turning point in the first awakening towards a more powerful and widespread proclamation of the gospel.

---

[8] Edwards' book can be found at http://www.iclnet.org/pub/resources/text/ipb-e/epl-10/web/edwards-narrative.html.

Edwards did not travel much, unlike George Tennent and George Whitefield. He faithfully pastored the church at Northampton for twenty-two years. He had a mediating effect in leading preachers and had opportunity to bring correction in both styles of preaching and in emotional excesses that came to increasingly be present in the awakening. He did not question all the emotions of those who were "wrought upon" by the Spirit but attempted to defend the awakening from various detractors.

Throughout his ministry, Edwards was wary of the "half-way covenant," and this eventually led to an unhappy departure from the church he loved so much. By a narrow vote, Edwards was dismissed, due to his insistence that only those who gave credible evidence of conversion should be accepted for church membership. So it was that America's greatest theologian, likely America's first biologist and first psychologist as well, and the courageous pastor whose preaching ushered in America's first awakening, was asked to leave his church. He remained in the town for a short while and preached at the church until the town's leaders forbade it. On July 1, 1750, he preached his last sermon at Northampton. Having few options and little resources, he and his wife with their ten children relocated to the encampment of the Housatonic Indians, where he served as a missionary for six years. In 1757, President Aaron Burr (father of Aaron Burr, vice-president under Thomas Jefferson and the one who also shot and killed Alexander Hamilton) of Princeton College died, and Edwards, who was President Burr's father-in-law, was invited to replace him. Not long after his inauguration, he submitted to receiving a small pox inoculation as a way of promoting the medical procedure, but he died as a result of it on March 22, 1758. Edwards's ministry continues more strongly than ever through accounts of his life and publication of his words.

George Whitefield—the Great Awakener

Whitefield was the "Methodist" preacher—Anglican actually, but a member of the Methodists at Oxford University with Charles and John Wesley, and so the label.[9]

Born in 1714, he lived in Gloucester, England, and his first job was working in the inn and tavern his father owned and operated. He had a large and wonderful speaking voice and thought about becoming an actor. In fact, he did study for the theater and no doubt used some of that training in his preaching. He has been called the greatest preacher the Church has ever known and may have preached to larger crowds than any other preacher in history, sometimes estimated at 30,000. Due to the size of the crowds gathered to hear him preach and the fact that many ministers denied him access to their churches, he became one of the first to preach out of doors as a regular procedure.

One of Whitefield's admirers was Benjamin Franklin, who loved to hear his friend preach. Sometimes against Franklin's will, or so he said, he would give money to Whitefield for the Georgia orphanage Whitefield had founded and continually promoted. It was said that Franklin would empty his pockets before hearing Whitefield preach, because he could not refrain from making financial contributions. Franklin thought highly of Whitefield, heard him gladly, yet never moved away from his deistic position to true Christian faith.

Whitefield had experienced a dramatic, if not traumatic, conversion experience while attending the "holy club" of the Methodists at Oxford. Few have been made so aware of personal sin and been made to see the awful eternal consequences of the wages of that sin as George Whitefield. After reading an account of the Spirit's hand upon Whitefield during that period, it seemed to me that he was very nearly driven mad. Later on

---

9 For an account of the lives of John and Charles Wesley, see *The Two Wesleys*, by Charles Haddon Spurgeon, 1861, published by Pilgrim Publications, Pasadena, Texas; and Iain H. Murray's *Wesley and Men Who Followed*, published in 2003 by Banner of Truth Trust.

in the awakening, his experience would prove helpful to him. As he witnessed the torment that sinners would go through when the Holy Spirit convicted them of sin, judgment, and righteousness, and as he would be confronted with charges that his preaching was driving people insane, memories of his own wrenching conversion experience steadied him. Indeed, some of those who heard Whitefield preach would be carried off to asylums.

In 1739, Whitefield came first to the middle colonies, then eventually to Philadelphia. There he met William Tennent, Sr., and a working relationship was established with the Log College preachers, especially Gilbert Tennent, with whom Whitefield was much impressed. Later on, Whitefield invited Gilbert to come along behind him as he made his preaching tours, and some said that Gilbert Tennent was a better preacher than Whitefield. Both shared a rather negative view of local clergy, particularly those considered to be among the Old Lights. In fact, the sermon that Gilbert Tennent became known for was *The Danger of an Unconverted Ministry.* One interesting peculiarity was that when Whitefield preached, people would characteristically be converted during the preaching. With Tennent, it was noted that often conversion would come afterward, sometimes days afterward.

Gilbert Tennent and his brothers were far more enthusiastic than was Whitefield, who mostly observed the manners he had learned as an Anglican priest. But the Tennents would be given to visions and other "charismatic" expressions. Gilbert, along with Whitefield, would earn the scorn of many of the Old Lights, by harping on the lack of Christian faith of those who opposed the awakening. In some quarters this was having a dampening effect on the revival, and Jonathan Edwards had occasion to address the issue with his fellow preachers. Whitefield did not take Edwards' admonitions well at first and complained about his fellow preacher's apparent stance against the work of God, but Whitefield later changed course and softened his pronouncements against the Old Lights, as did Tennent.

Whitefield's preaching generated much excitement, and newspapers in Philadelphia began to take interest as well. Full texts of his sermons were published in the newspapers, and friends of the awakening printed up the sermons into evangelistic tracts.

Throughout the awakening, reports of it would find their way into the publications of the time. The revival preachers were often the objects of the news themselves. Newspapers called Gilbert Tennent a "holy necromancer" and generally implied that he was a careful and calculating magician. Largely this was because few had ever before witnessed the powerful moving of the Holy Spirit.

Few preached like Whitefield, and his preaching was entertainment to many. The media coverage became what Edwards might have called "means" as many traveled long distances to hear him. "Means" meant that the preachers used gimmicks or tricks in their work, and thus the means produced the conversions rather than the sovereign work of God.

Leaving Philadelphia, Whitefield visited Elizabethtown, New Jersey, and preached at Jonathan Dickinson's church. Dickinson became the first president of what later became Princeton College, and in 1741 he preached a sermon titled *The Theology of New Birth,* which I consider one of the finest sermons to come out of the awakening. In *Are You Really Born Again?* the full sermon is placed in the appendix, with my paraphrase of it found within the body of the book itself.[10]

At the outset, Whitefield was locked out of or denied access to most churches, so he continued what he had done in his home country of England and began preaching outdoors. The Old Lights thought this irregular, and it contributed to their negative view of the awakening generally and Whitefield's methods in particular. For many years Whitefield preached

---

10   Published by Evangelical Press in 1998, second edition in 2005

in the colonies long after the generally understood period of the awakening had ceased, right up until his death on September 30, 1770, in Newburyport, Massachusetts of a supposed asthma attack. After preaching into the night, he retired to a friend's house, but so many people desired to hear him just a little bit more, that Whitefield complied. Finally exhausted, he withdrew to his bedroom and died early that morning.

Whitefield made seven trips across the Atlantic. Three of the seven of Whitefield's trips were made after the awakening was largely over, in 1754, 1764, and 1770, the year of his death. For thirty years the "great awakener" worked tirelessly as an evangelist. He preached to perhaps the largest crowds, without amplification, in the history of the Church. He may have been the greatest preacher who ever lived. He made his mistakes, particularly in the early years while he was working closely with Gilbert Tennent; and though he was stung by the corrective words of Edwards and others, he realized his excesses and changed. By the end of his work, Whitefield was considered by many to be the apostle to the English speaking world, in much the same way as Paul was the apostle to the Gentiles.

The beginnings of Evangelicalism?

The conversion experience of the Anglican George Whitefield while attending Oxford University occurred outside the mediating ministry of the Church of England. Though a communicant member of the state church, baptized and confirmed, he did not experience the new birth until undergoing a rather extreme sense of personal guilt followed by release and relief as he found peace with God. As a result, and without question, his means of grace did not come through the agency of the church.

Even the colonial Puritans relied on a mediated salvation that was facilitated by the family and the church. Whitefield's ministry saw conversions taking place outside the ministrations of the church. While he preached the gospel, people were converted. Many of these later presented themselves to churches to request baptism and membership, but it was after the fact.

Whitefield's preaching was rooted in a rather simple and clear evangelical message—a call to trust in Jesus Christ for forgiveness of sin and for salvation. The saving agent was Christ alone and mediated only through the transforming power of the Holy Spirit. Those who imitated this as yet unnamed evangelicalism were the Methodists and the Baptists, especially the Baptists.

Dark side of the first awakening

"Wild fire revival" or "dark sides of revival"—these are basically synonymous terms. It is no secret and no real scandal that awakenings have always, probably must always, see circumstances and events that detract from the general and overall work of God. Jonathan Edwards devoted particular attention to this in his *Distinguishing Marks of the Work of the Spirit of God*, a summary of which is found in the appendix to this book. Edwards wrote his book to honor God for that which he saw as genuine and defended it against various detractors. Sadly, most of the denigrating of the awakening came from within the Christian community.

Gilbert Tennent's sermon, *The Danger of an Unconverted Ministry*, stirred up some considerable opposition from the Old Lights, those ministers who questioned the validity of the awakening right from its early days, due to so-called irregularities, such as preaching outdoors, preaching on other than the appointed days—Sundays and Wednesdays (usually), and ministers going into the parishes of others to hold preaching services. Then there were the so-called excesses—the noise, bodily movements, fainting, shouts for joy, and so on—all of which were normally absent in the churches of the time. Tennent's, and later on, James Davenport's charges against the Old Lights as being both unconverted and against the work of God produced an environment that cast religion as a whole into a bad light.

Aaron Burr, again the father of the Aaron Burr who killed Alexander Hamilton in a duel, wrote about the "radicals'" excesses. Burr listed them point by point: (1) Their being led by impulses & impressions; (2) Their giving heed to visions, trances, & revelations; (3) Their speaking of divine things with an air of levity & vanity, laughter & etc.; (4) Their declaring their judgment about others—whether they are converted or not; (5) Their making their own feelings a rule to judge others by; (6) For laymen to take upon themselves to exhort in a public assembly; (7) Their separating from their minister under a notion of his being unregenerate.[11]

James Davenport of Long Island was a preacher who began well but became a scandalous presence during the awakening, then reversed course again and apologized for his excesses. Whitefield thought much of Davenport's preaching and ministry early on and even recommended him. Perhaps thinking too highly of himself, Davenport violated one of Colonial America's unwritten laws, that of preaching in the parishes of other ministers without being invited. He was given to having *impressions* of a spiritual nature, or so he thought, thus claiming certain spiritual authority without being held accountable to biblical correctness. After the fashion of Gilbert Tennent, he took up the practice of denouncing the growing number of those who criticized him as being unconverted. But Davenport went so far as to advise members to leave their churches if he was convinced they were led by unconverted ministers. He further called them to become his own followers. Tennent had done the same, but in a milder, more gentlemanly fashion than Davenport.

---

11 This is quoted from *The Great Awakening* by Thomas S. Kidd, pages 142-143, published by Yale University Press in 2007, a most valuable and important history of the Great Awakening.

For several years Davenport created confusion and caused division in some congregations, until finally he was censored and his ministry restricted by the Connecticut legislature in 1742. That same body actually arrested him, declared him to be insane, and sent him home. This did not stop him, however, as he continued his strange behavior in Boston. He was arrested and convicted once more but won release by being one of the first to use the defense of mental incompetence.

After forming a church in New London, Connecticut, Davenport went on to further embarrass the leaders of the awakening by claiming to have received commands from God. This was in addition to the strange bodily postures he displayed, along with making sounds like that of a wild animal. In New London he collected books written by some of the great Puritan writers, along with various articles of clerical garb, and burned them. With this, Davenport's fanaticism began to fade, and he recovered his right mind, published a confession of his antics as error, and asked for forgiveness. He recognized that what he thought was instruction from God—the *impressions*—were, in fact, not godly at all. However, it was too late for those who had become skeptical of the awakening—the damage had been done. The newspapers had covered the entire debacle, and the general public did not change its mind. In addition, Davenport's followers did not alter their course, they merely left him behind and continued down the same unhappy road. Some of the "separatist" churches that had looked to Davenport for leadership eventually returned to their original denomination or joined with the Baptists.

Charles Chauncy, the Congregationalist pastor of the First Church, or *Old Brick Church*, probably the most famous minister in New England, became the unofficial leader of the Old Lights. To one degree or another, these ministers opposed the awakening. (I have wondered, given the excesses of some parts of the awakening, if I would not have identified with the Old Lights rather than the New.) It was not so much a question of liberal versus conservative; it had much to do with ministerial protocol and decorum. Chauncy particularly attacked the new manner of preaching, which was done with greater emotion and less classical style than was customary. Forms of preaching varied, of course. Jonathan Edwards conformed to the accepted means of preaching, meaning that he read out his sermons with little display of emotion; but Whitefield, Tennent, and Davenport, among others, departed from the accepted norms. Despite this, I think it can be said that those interested in the awakening valued genuine conversion to be of greater importance than adherence to accepted styles of preaching.

In response to Jonathan Edwards' 1740 book, *Thoughts on the Revival of Religion in New England*, Chauncy wrote *Seasonable Thoughts on the State of Religion in New England*, in which he chronicled what he considered to be the excesses of the awakening and essentially condemned the whole as not being of the Spirit of God. The defenders of the awakening directly responded to Chauncy's charges and did admit to irregularities, especially in regard to bodily movements and the *impressions* of some. Under the preaching of Whitefield, the Tennents, and Edwards to a much lesser degree, there were questionable expressions of religious enthusiasm by some, but not anywhere to the extent to be found later in the second awakening, especially in the camp meetings, which will be noted in the next chapter.

It must have been quite a time in New England—Chauncy verses Edwards— and Davenport's excesses made things worse for Edwards who was condemningly painted with a broad brush stroke of *enthusiasm* by Chauncy. Chauncy declared that he favored a tempered and reasonable evangelism, a "real and effectual renovation of heart and life."[12]

---

12   Larry Witham, *A City Upon a Hill: How Sermons Changed the Course of American History* (New York: HarperCollins Publishers, 2007), 55.

Chauncy's sermon *Enthusiasm Described and Cautioned Against* was directed at Davenport's behavior in particular and the whole awakening in general. The sermons by both preachers found their way into newspapers and made for some lively entertainment. But even while the awakening was fading away, Edwards continued with his strong preaching, the very preaching that eventually led to his being dismissed from his church in Northampton. In fact, the more Edwards saw of the awakening, and the more he had to examine it in light of the attacks against it, the more Calvinistic his preaching and his theology became. Dr. Chauncy, the reasonable and established pastor of the most important church in New England, was a formidable foe, and it was his views that eventually prevailed, at least in New England.

A greater number of faithful Christians

The preceding is a radically truncated history of the first awakening. Many other faithful Christians engaged in preaching and pastoral ministries and were part of the awakening. These became largely unknown to the broader sweep of history, but their faithfulness may have been recorded in the records of small churches scattered throughout the colonies. It is also typical of awakenings that some preachers and evangelists are used of God for a period of time, perhaps in large ways, but then fade back into the ordinary affairs of life. God pours out his Spirit on some for a while, and then it seems as if that anointing is withdrawn. This is what we experienced in the JPM as well. People I know to this day were suddenly much engaged in the awakening that is called the Jesus People Movement, who had been complete unknowns to that point, and then when normal times returned they went back to their normal lives.

There were faithful Christians who longed for renewal, prayed for it, and did what they could to promote it—most of whom never saw an answer to their prayers or fruit from their work. Did that great awakening come in response to the prayers for renewal? This cannot be answered one way or the other. This is what Christians do: we pray, plan, and preach for revival and awakening. And should the Spirit be poured out, we can only say, "Thank you, Lord" and not make any effort to claim influence.

Impact of the Great Awakening

No precise means of measuring the results or impact of an awakening exist. Perhaps the best measure would be to see how many new converts joined churches, or answered an altar call, or requested baptism—but with this awakening, as with most, we can only make wild guesses.

Probably most of those who were converted were already church members and would therefore already have been baptized. There were no altar calls, or coming forward, or sinner's prayers to be repeated—these *means* would not be invented until the 1820s, essentially. That large crowds attended the preaching, especially to hear George Whitefield, is well known. Estimates of nearly 30,000 seem to be the highest number ever to hear him speak.

Edwards puts the number of converted at Northampton at three hundred, and these were mostly existing congregants. In any case, the largest possible number of those affected would be small by modern standards, because of the rather small population of the colonies at the time—about one million at best. There was spiritual and moral renewal, there were conversions, and the colonial society did benefit—this much the historians tell us. Some taverns closed, some theaters also closed; Edwards said that youth were no longer so engaged in *frolics,* and there was a focus on eternal things. Jesus and eternity became much a part of everyday conversation. It might be that a generation became spiritually and morally strong enough to raise the next generation who would face the great trial that was to come—the American Revolution.

There are some statistics, however. The Congregationalists saw substantial growth. In New England, with a population of around 350,000, the awakening resulted in 150 new churches, bringing the total to 530. It is estimated that from 25,000 to 50,000 people joined churches during the awakening. (Notice the wide range in the numbers.) In the Middle Colonies, the Presbyterians benefited significantly. One measure of note is that the number of Presbyterian ministers increased from 45 to more than 100 between 1740 and 1760. Baptists, who did not immediately endorse the awakening but often stood apart, grew the most. In New England they grew from 21 to 79 churches in the same time frame of 1740 to 1760. The awakening laid the foundation for what would shortly become a dramatic growth of Baptists in the southern colonies. The Episcopal Church, direct cousin to the Anglican Church of Great Britain, mostly remained part of the opposition, despite the presence of one of their own, George Whitefield. They did, however, benefit from the awakening later.

Besides numbers, the awakening stimulated the establishment of educational institutions and missionary work, particularly to American Indians. To train the leaders needed for the new churches, schools were founded that later became identified as "ivy league" institutions.

Somewhat of an intangible effect, but often mentioned by historians, was the growth in the concept of religious freedom, which would translate itself into libertarian ideas in general. With the rise of non-established denominations like the Baptists or even with the presence of the so-called "separatists" (those groups who did not easily fit into existing mainline colonial denominations), a new tolerance for diversity was thrust upon the colonial population. There now existed persons who did not worship in the colonies' established churches, such as Anglican (Episcopal), Presbyterian, Congregational, and Quaker. Now there were people with different ideas and practices who were not easily controlled or managed. Freedom of expression was coming, and cooperation among diverse groups of different denominational churches was appearing.

The uniqueness of awakenings

The second awakening, to which we now turn our attention, was quite unlike the first. The third would be different still, and the Jesus People Movement would also be unique. Yet they each shared common characteristics: one, they began and they ended, though the exact dates are ill-defined; two, many persons were converted, many more so than during other normal times; three, the means of conversion was the preached gospel of Jesus Christ; four, there was an increased interest in things eternal, in Jesus Christ and his cross, in Bible study and prayer, in observing the central Christian traditions of baptism and the Lord's Supper; five, biblical ethics and morals re-emerged; six, controversy, division, and aberrant expressions of religion sprang up; seven, the awakening times were and will be remembered for generations as being unusual and powerful.

Two:
The second awakening in America (a.1798 - a.1835)

It was fifty-six years between the early signs of the decline of the First Great Awakening and the start of the second, in the opinion of the majority of historians. Localized awakenings did not cease during that time. Commenting on that interim period Frank Beardsley wrote in *A History of American Revivals*, "At no time since the Great Awakening had revivals wholly ceased."[13] The notion that 1742 started the decline of the first awakening would have been challenged by George Whitefield, who continued to preach until his death in 1770 and who did see many conversions during that period. Other contemporaries of Whitefield, also active during those years, might also question the date normally given for the decline or ending of that revival time. In *The Great Awakening* Thomas S. Kidd has concluded that the first two awakenings were actually one single awakening:

> This book has shown that there was a First Great Awakening, but it was a long Great Awakening and produced a new variation of Protestant Christianity: evangelicalism. Although revivals were an essential part of the new movement, their frequent absence between 1735

---
13 Frank Beardsley, *A History of American Revivals* (New York: American Tract Society, 1912), 84.

and 1785 did not signal the termination of the movement.[14]

Dr. Kidd describes localized awakenings that took place in the 1760s, 1780s, and times in between, that he says demonstrate that the awakening begun in 1735 had never ceased. For Kidd, then, the First Great Awakening stretched from 1735 to 1835, a hundred year period.

Perhaps Kidd is correct, and he is not alone in his view as I have described it above. However, much may depend on what makes an awakening something distinct from what occurs normally. To be designated an awakening, it seems necessary that it must be widespread, suddenly appearing, and just as suddenly ceasing, with conversions to Christ as the central phenomenon rather than simply a series of exciting and enthusiastic gatherings. The outpourings Kidd presents in chapters fifteen, sixteen, and seventeen of his excellent *The Great Awakening* would not be considered special or unique. Such times of revival are constantly going on somewhere in the world. Additionally, some of that which Kidd describes in the above-mentioned chapters may have been something other than an outpouring of the Holy Spirit, since evangelists had by that time learned to humanly engineer what may have passed as true awakenings but were, in fact, something less.

Dating the awakening

Dates given for awakenings are merely estimates, and so it is with America's second awakening. A reliable beginning date may be 1798, or maybe 1799, maybe even 1800 or earlier, as there are indications, as previously stated, that there were isolated and small awakenings cropping up in various places ever since 1742. In 1790, small revivals were reported in diverse parts of the country, where churches were revived

---

14 Thomas S. Kidd, *The Great Awakening: The Roots of Evangelical Christianity in Colonial America* (New Haven, CT: Yale University Press, 2007), 322-323.

and non-believers converted, and these appeared to develop independent of one another. Here and there, this preacher and that preacher, Presbyterian, Congregational, Baptist, Methodist—awakenings were reported, especially in parts of Virginia and Georgia. Still the outpourings came through preaching in established churches, as in the first awakening. Then in New England, particularly Boston at the First Baptist Church, there were stirrings of the Spirit noticeable in 1790. Two years later at Lee, Massachusetts, under the ministry of Alvin Hyde, there was a considerable revival. Edward Dorr Griffin, whose ministry in New England had a great impact, testified that from 1792 to 1799 he saw continual awakening. For the most part, the preachers or evangelists are unknown, their names gone from general history; no Edwards or Whitefield—simply Reverend or Pastor so and so.

The second outpouring, as generally understood, may be divided into two distinct parts: one, roughly from 1798 to 1825, and the second, from 1825 to 1835. Again, these dates are open to debate. Much of the differences in dating have to do with Charles G. Finney, whose evangelistic work began to expand from 1825 to 1830.

J. Edwin Orr, in his most useful book on the awakening of 1857-58, *The Event of the Century,* notes that the two phases of the second awakening were so different, that some recognized them as two awakenings not one. "Contemporary analysts of the 1857-58 Revival recognized four major awakenings, 1734 onward, 1797 onward, 1830 onward, and 1857-58."[15] Some historians, then, at the time of the 1857-58 awakening thought it should be designated a fourth awakening. They counted as the first awakening that which had begun with Edwards in 1734; they saw the second beginning in 1797 and ending with the onset of Finney's work; a third awakening came under Finney; and a fourth covered those years of 1857-

---

15   J. Edwin Orr, *The Event of the Century*, Richard Owen Roberts, ed. (Wheaton, IL: International Awakening Press, 1989), xiv-xv.

58. It is this last period that I designate as the third awakening in this writing. However accurate this evaluation may be, and to a large extent I agree with it, the consensus of histories of awakenings identifies only three American awakenings. We cannot fail to note, however, that Finney's ministry radically changed the face of American evangelical Christianity.

The age of reason

The years between the awakenings saw the growth of deism, universalism, and Unitarianism, with Unitarianism rising directly out of established and orthodox Christian denominations, especially the Congregational Church, in which Stoddard and Edwards held their ordinations. Ethan Allen's *Reason the Only Oracle of Man* and Thomas Paine's *The Age of Reason* attacked the foundations of revealed religious truth and championed human reason. Thomas Jefferson's deist concepts influenced many hearts and minds. The paradoxes of Christianity—the Trinity, the deity and humanity of Jesus Christ, the human and divine origins of the Bible, and the mysteries of election—being beyond the ability of the natural mind to comprehend, caused many to reject general Christian doctrine outright. The expansion of political freedoms brought with it freedom of religion, as it should, and the door was open to safely reject the authority of the Christian churches. Along with the rejection of biblical authority, moral restraint suffered as well, and the general but gradual decline was apparent to those who cared.

The years leading up to the second awakening remind me of the years following the Jesus People Movement to this present day. There has been an observable, measureable movement away from Christianity toward Eastern religions, notably Buddhism, and toward practical atheism, despite the appearance of the mega-church and the church growth movement as a whole. However, there is not anything really new or different in this; only the names of the groups have changed. Spiritual movements are usually toward unbelief and a rejection of and a rebellion against the God of the Judaeo-Christian Scripture.

On the eve of the second awakening

At least as early as 1795 reports of outpourings of the Spirit began surfacing that were reminiscent of the "harvests" Solomon Stoddard experienced during the years leading up to the general, wider outpouring in and around 1734. It must be noted that, as is true for all genuine awakenings, outpourings of the Spirit came up rather suddenly and in a number of places at once or close in time to one another. And there was nothing humanly organized about them, except that concerned believers were engaged in praying for revival and pastors preached for the need for revival. Perhaps this is how awakenings begin—Christians having the sense that they ought to pray for and preach about the need for God's Spirit to be poured out.

The praying and the preaching were the "means" used, and these were nothing new or dramatic, merely ordinary. This also is how awakenings are identified—unusual outpourings with no unusual means used. Iain H. Murray writes:

> What characterizes a revival is not the employment of unusual or special means but rather the extraordinary degree of blessing attending the normal means of grace. There were no announcements of pending revivals. Pastors were simply continuing in the services they had conducted for many years when the great change began. That is why so many of them could say, "The first appearance of the work was sudden and unexpected."[16]

---

16   Iain H. Murray, *Revival and Revivalism,* page 129.

The awakening in the West

Though the description of the awakening in the West will be our starting point here, that is not an indication that the West was the birthplace of the awakening; origins are unknown. "West" for this time period refers to Kentucky, Tennessee, Georgia, the Carolinas, and surrounding territories. At the time of the first awakening, the population of America was just under one million. By 1800, another million people had moved westward from the old colonial states. The migrants left their churches behind, while preachers and pastors followed more slowly. In that interim, a typical and general decline in morals and spirituality took place. Christians who were troubled by these events prayed for God to remedy the situation, prompting some preachers to venture out to the frontier.

James McGready (1762-1817), along with Barton Stone and William McGee, both of whom McGready had influenced, were preaching in the Western frontier, and the awakening in that raw region caught on fire with the sparks of their gospel proclamations. With bold declarations of sin and grace, heaven and hell, judgment and mercy, these preachers aroused the new settlers through the "camp meetings," as they came to be called by 1802. (Another term for "camp meeting" current at the time was "brush arbor meeting.") The first camp meeting, in June of 1800, was organized by McGready and attended mostly by members of the three small Presbyterian churches he pastored in Logan County, Kentucky. The early camp meetings highlighted "communion season"—the Lord's Supper held outdoors—with preaching preceding the communion. In a short time, Congregationalists, Methodists, and Baptists joined with the Presbyterians, and the meetings were termed "General Camp Meetings."

Camp meetings met many needs. Family and friends had often been left behind in the move west, and familiar forms of society were nearly non-existent, but the camp meetings brought people together. They were a great deal of fun—sometimes too much fun.

The Gasper River and Cane Ridge camp meetings (in 1801) were much larger than the initial one under the ministry of McGready. People by the thousands came from great distances to attend. For days and weeks, people gathered to celebrate communion from predominantly Presbyterian, Methodist, and Baptist preachers and to hear strong and long gospel sermons. And the Spirit was poured out as many, eventually thousands, experienced conviction of their sin and then "found peace" in trusting in Christ as Savior.

It was at the Cane Ridge, Kentucky meeting, August 1801, under the preaching of Presbyterian Barton Stone (1772-1844), that the full power of the awakening first became evident. People arrived from nearby states, and the crowd was estimated to be between 10,000 and 25,000. It was said that everyone sang the same songs, all united in prayer, and all the preachers of the various denominations preached the same message—salvation in Jesus Christ. The ministers were in agreement that it was a genuine work of God, despite irregularities.

Awakenings generally begin orderly and without much excess. The ministers themselves usually seem to determine the presence and the extent of the excesses. The emergence of excesses is characteristic of a movement from revival to revivalism. In the West, Iain Murray points out that the excesses began in June of 1800 at the Red River Church in Kentucky, when Methodist John McGee from Tennessee thought that disorderly outcries were evidence of the power of God.[17] Once the door to revivalism was open, it was almost impossible to close it.

The excesses were often termed "exercises," and it was argued by those who were offended by them that they "profited little." It is probable that in 1 Timothy 4:8, Paul is not speaking

---
17 Ibid., 164.

of the type of behavior exhibited at the camp meetings but rather was referring to athletic training or exercising. Many ministers thought that the bodily movements—falling to the ground, dancing, barking, jerking of the whole body, and so on—were an indication that God was in their midst, so they therefore encouraged the exercises. Those ministers who tried were sometimes able to minimize or even eliminate the exercises altogether.

The exercises could be of short duration, or they could last for days. Skeptics among those gathered at the camp meetings who attempted to avoid the oncoming of the exercises were often not able to withstand them. When the exercises came upon a meeting, the noise and confusion could drown out the preaching of the gospel.

But then again, there is evidence that those who succumbed to the exercises, even the jerks, would have their attention drawn to the extent of their sin and the urgent need of forgiveness and of trusting Christ as Savior. The exercises therefore yielded some good result. It is not a simple thing to ferret out exactly what transpired in the camp meetings, and this I found also to be true of the Jesus People Movement. God is, after all, in control of genuine awakening, and he can bring good out of even that which is plainly error.

On the other hand, the camp meetings could be completely orderly and peaceful; and this was especially true when the focus was on the Lord's Supper.

The designation "camp meeting" has a certain taint to it; even to this day there is something of the wild and enthusiastic associated with the term. Early on, especially under the administration of the Presbyterians and Baptists, the meetings tended to be well-ordered and sober. As time went on this changed, particularly with the Methodists, and the name of the Methodist Peter Cartwright is the one most associated with the camp meetings.

Cartwright (1785-1872) was one of the great preachers on the American frontier and founded churches all over the West. He was a Methodist circuit rider who reportedly baptized 10,000 people and preached 15,000 sermons in Tennessee and Kentucky. His temperament was ideal for the American frontier of that era. He was a rough and ready fighter in every way. He fought sin and the Baptists every chance he could get. He especially argued against baptism by immersion, which had always been a hallmark of Baptist doctrine. He also denounced Reformed/Calvinistic theology in favor of his Methodist version of Arminianism. After a long career preaching throughout the American frontier, because of his distaste for slavery, he moved to Illinois where he became involved in politics. In 1846 he ran against Abraham Lincoln for congress but lost.

Stoddard to Edwards to Dwight—
the awakening in the East

Solomon Stoddard was the grandfather of Jonathan Edwards, who was an important personage of the first American awakening; Jonathan Edwards was the grandfather of Timothy Dwight, who figured prominently in the second American awakening. The impact of that one family was significant, perhaps incalculable.

Timothy Dwight was a leader in the second awakening as it occurred in New England. In 1795 he was chosen president of Yale College, having served as a chaplain during the War of Independence. Yale was founded as a college to train ministers, but in 1795, Dwight was certain there was little true Christianity among the students. He then set about to change this condition. His expressions of genuine caring for the students, his strong, clear, helpful sermons, and his consistent prayer for God to turn the institution around to His glory yielded results. In 1802, first a few students came under conviction, then nearly all the student body experienced conversion or awakening. With the good news coming out of Yale, awakening spread to other colleges and to the New England churches in general.

Dwight's manner was serious, as his grandfather's had been, and he was also careful that none of the excesses sometimes associated with that first awakening manifest themselves at Yale. Jonathan Edwards had written extensively on the various forms of enthusiasm of that earlier period, and since Dwight was well aware of these writings, he vowed to prevent any stain from attaching itself to the awakening current in his own time.

Of great significance, however, was the way in which Dwight understood awakenings, a view that would mark and actually come to characterize most evangelical Christianity around the world to the present day. Dwight thought that awakenings could be produced by human effort. He knew that his grandfather's and his great, great grandfather's theology would not so allow, but Dwight set out to create an awakening much like those his forbearers experienced. These forbearers thought that the sovereign God brought awakening and conversions according to His good pleasure alone, totally uninfluenced by any human agency. Dwight, however, placed a good deal of emphasis on human choice; after all, this was the age of reason, an age when human capacity seemed nearly unlimited. Could it be that Dwight was influenced by his culture? If so, it would not be unprecedented.

While Stoddard and Edwards would certainly have argued that a sovereign God brought awakening utterly apart from anything humans might do, including prayer, Dwight thought there might be a cooperation between God and man—a synergism. He thought that Christians ought to pray, plan, and preach for awakening and that they could undoubtedly produce it by those means. Stoddard and Edwards would have argued that such cooperation gave humans too much ability, given the tragic consequences of the Fall, and that if cooperation were the central dynamic between God and humans, then humans would ultimately be in control. Timothy Dwight's views represented what might be called a *paradigm shift*.

The stage was then set for what was to come under Charles Finney's influence—revival that could be humanly engineered. However, Finney took the Dwight idea much further, claiming and teaching that people could actually decide to become Christians, a sharp break from the prevailing Calvinism as expressed by men like Asahel Nettleton.

Asahel Nettleton

The Rev. Asahel Nettleton from Connecticut (1783-1844) was the most notable evangelist of the first half of the second awakening. Licensed to preach by the Congregationalists of New Haven in 1811, his hope was to be a missionary. His preaching style was reminiscent of the Puritan tradition he had inherited, in that he was reserved and dignified in the pulpit, much like Jonathan Edwards had been. Also like Edwards, his preaching resulted in scores of conversions, perhaps as many as 30,000 over the course of his ministry. His was the time-honored method of presenting clearly and forcefully the person and work of Jesus Christ and the necessity of repenting of sin and trusting Jesus as Savior and Lord. The gospel was preached; the results would then lie with the Holy Spirit. More will be said about this particular point, because it is an issue of great importance.

Nettleton observed the normal protocols of his time, conducting services only at the established times and preaching outside of his own area only upon invitation. He never married, lived a simple life, would not charge any fees for his ministry, and emphasized the need to disciple new converts. He enjoyed close fellowship with a number of other preachers in New England, chief among whom were Lyman Beecher, Edward Payson, Edward Dorr Griffin, and Gardiner Spring. The lives and work of these men are well worth investigation, yet with the exception of Lyman Beecher, little is known of them today. Iain H. Murray does discuss these men in *Revival and Revivalism.*

Nettleton, among others, questioned Finney's "new measures," especially the various techniques Finney used to obtain immediate decisions to accept Christ. Finney did preach Christ, but it was what followed that troubled Nettleton. William R. Weeks, an associate of Lyman Beecher's, expressed the objections that he and others, including Asahel Nettleton, had to the new measures employed by Finney:

> We complain that the whole system of measures seems to be adapted to promote false conversions, to cherish false hopes, and propagate a false religion; and thus, ultimately, not only destroy the souls of those who are deceived by it, but to bring revivals, and experimental religion itself, into discredit.[18]

The intramural debate between the Christian evangelists was newsworthy in that era and was widely publicized in the newspapers and magazines of the time. Nettleton, never strong physically, gradually lost the debate to Finney. Finney was exciting, and his converts could be counted—much unlike Nettleton. The result is felt across the globe today.[19]

Charles Finney and the second half of the second awakening

Some argue that the second awakening was over by the time Charles G. Finney (1792-1875) began his evangelistic

---

[18] William R. Weeks, *The Pilgrim's Progress in the Nineteenth Century* (New York, 1848), as found in Murray, *Revival and Revivalism*, 242.

[19] It was the reading of the debate over the new measures that began in 1826 between Charles Finney and Asahel Nettleton that first attracted my attention to Reformed/Calvinistic theology. For the first time in my life I began to understand the differences between the two concepts, especially as they impacted evangelistic methodology and caused me to question my own form of evangelism. For many years as a pastor I taught, chapter by chapter, Finney's *Revival Lectures* and *Revivals of Religion.*

preaching in the 1820s. Asahel Nettleton might have made the argument, or at least he would have thought that Finney had distorted the awakening that was then in progress.

Finney was converted in 1821, not without some considerable struggling, and his chief issue was "whether he should accept Jesus Christ as his Savior, or continue the pursuit of a worldly life."[20] From the very outset of his Christian life, Finney held to the dual concepts that becoming a Christian somehow lay within human ability while at the same time salvation was a gift of grace and not obtainable by works.[21] This theology had been preached by the early Methodist circuit riders such as Francis Asbury, whose views were gaining ground among American Calvinists.

Finney, a trained lawyer, was admitted to the bar in New York. He was converted and tutored under the ministry of Rev. George W. Gale, a graduate of Princeton, who taught what might be called a hyper form of Calvinism. Finney was licensed to preach in March of 1824 by the Presbyterians and developed further the understandings of revival held by Timothy Dwight. Whereas Gale taught a Calvinistic theology, where a sovereign God did all the work of salvation through election, Finney would teach and practice that revivals could be created and conversions could be secured by what would come to be called "new measures." One of these was the mourner's bench or anxious seat, used to bring people to an immediate decision for Christ and to publicly commit themselves to serving Christ as Lord. These measures were not meant to manipulate people into becoming Christians but were thought of as legitimate mechanisms to be used by the Christian evangelist. The new measures began to appear in Finney's meetings after

---

20 Beardsley, 118.
21 Finney had been influenced by the writings of Nathaniel W. Taylor, (1786-1858) who departed from his Calvinistic background by advancing the idea that human beings have the capacity to determine their salvation. Taylor, identified with the New Haven Theology, shared much of same theological ground as the Methodist movement that was having more and more impact on American evangelicalism.

approximately six years of evangelistic work—but they had been in his mind for some years previously. It is probable that Finney only refined and adopted on a larger scale methods with which he had already become acquainted.

Finney had at some point, then, determined that it was humanly possible to make a decision to become a Christian. Finney believed that each person had the ability to repent and believe while yet in his or her sin, contrary to Reformed ways of thinking. "He insisted, the Holy Spirit works through means and instrumentalities, and if these are made use of as prescribed by the Word of God, the Holy Spirit will use them in the conversion of men."[22]

According to Finney, repentance and believing came before conversion. Reformed theology taught that repentance and faith were produced by the Holy Spirit only after regeneration or the new birth. (Calvinistic preaching included both a call to turn from sin and believe in Jesus as well as an emphasis on the sovereign electing work of God.) Nettleton would have questioned the efficacy of decision-making, wondering whether the result would be a false rather than a true conversion. It is probable that Finney is responsible for a form of the well-known "sinner's prayer," now employed as a standard mechanism for supposedly becoming a Christian.

By at least 1835, Finney knew that he had departed from the general orthodox theology of conversion and talked of it openly. According to Finney, he had recovered, if not invented, the genuine theology of conversion. Finney was convinced that conversion was the result of human decision, not a miracle work of God, and that the preacher's responsibility was to induce that decision.

Finney was a grand preacher—forceful, brilliant, fearless, and articulate. He appealed to all levels of society. Though he was not compared to George Whitefield, Finney nevertheless became renowned as an evangelist, especially in the New

---
22   Ibid., 149.

York area. It is estimated that 500,000 were converted over the course of his ministry. As time went on, well past the date of 1835 usually set for the ending of the second awakening, Finney continued to preach and continued to abandon Reformed thought. He completely embraced a human-centered gospel, well beyond what is normally held by Arminian theologians. In 1832, after prolonged tension with his ordaining body, Finney connected with the Congregationalists.

Toward the end of Finney's ministry, he admitted that the resulting conversions from his evangelistic campaigns were less than what had been originally reported and claimed. Finney is quoted as saying, in referring to converts under his preaching, that "the great body of them are a disgrace to religion."[23] Finney thought the reason for this was an improper view he held in regard to sanctification. His rationale was as follows: "I was often instrumental in bringing Christians under great conviction and into a state of temporary repentance and faith but, falling short of urging them up to a point where they would become so acquainted with Christ as to abide in him, they would of course soon relapse again into their former state."[24]

It might be a sounder conclusion that his decision-based evangelism resulted in false conversion or Christianization rather than true conversion. And this had been the very concern of Asahel Nettleton.

One last point may be made in regard to the influence Finney had on evangelical Christianity in America. Toward the end of his active evangelistic work he read a book by John Wesley titled *Plain Account of Christian Perfection*. Wesley, toward the end of his life, had begun to explore the possibility that a Christian might be able to attain to sinless perfection

---

23   Murray, *Revival and Revivalism*, 289.
24   Ibid.

in "a second, more mature stage of Christian life."[25] It would appear that Finney's conclusion that an insufficient sanctification was to blame for the lack of committed converts could be attributed to his reliance on Wesley's ideas.

Dark side of the second awakening

The awakening in New England, from 1798 to the 1820s, was characterized by a freedom from the forms of enthusiasm that came to be associated with the awakening in the West. Indeed, it is possible that the first awakening of 1734-1742 was shortened, if not altogether concluded, by excesses of enthusiasm. High emotions, strong feelings, impulses, and impressions began to be expressed even under the ministry of Edwards, Whitefield, and the Tennents. It never is a simple matter to distinguish between what is produced by the Spirit of God and that which is coming from either the human spirit or a demonic spirit. This difficulty of discernment was also true of the Jesus People Movement and perhaps is true for every outpouring of the genuine Holy Spirit. After all, New Testament writers and Jesus himself warn of spiritual warfare and demonic deception.

The awakening in New England saw little use of the new measures, those techniques used to revive and obtain conversion decisions, like the anxious seat or standing or raising an arm to indicate acceptance of Christ, both often employed by Charles Finney. In New England the preaching services mostly took place in established houses of worship and during the regularly scheduled times. To some extent, it was church business as usual— ordinary, and not a camp meeting or series of special services that had their own built-in excitement. No, the attraction was merely the Word preached by pastors who were well-known and trusted. The theology of the sermons

---

25 See Mark A. Noll's account of this in his *A History of Christianity in the United States and Canada* (Grand Rapids, MI: William B. Eerdmans Publishing Company,1992), 235.

consisted, for the most part, of simple, straight-forward Reformed/Calvinistic doctrines. The manner in which conversions took place was similar to those that occurred in the first awakening. Frank Beardsley described the typical process of conversion in the New England awakenings:

> In most instances there was a period of distress during which the persons affected were sensible of the depravity of their hearts, their unworthiness before God, and a conviction that it would be just of God were he to cast them off forever. The transition from this state to one of joy and peace in believing would sometimes be sudden, but in other instances the convicted would be distressed for months before relief came.[26]

In the American West, it was at the Cane Ridge camp meeting that excesses first became evident. The first awakening, as previously stated, had its share of excess—impulses and impressions that some supposed were from the Holy Spirit, bodily movements that were not usual in church gatherings, and some visions and dreams of a spiritual nature assumed to have originated from God. All of these and more came to characterize the awakening in the West. As in the first awakening, there were efforts on the part of the ministers to tame the unusual, distracting behavior, and as in the first, there were those who wanted to encourage the "power of the Spirit." In the second awakening, excesses were not so quickly or easily corralled. As I read accounts of what went on at the camp meetings, especially Cane Ridge and following, I am reminded of 20th and 21st Century American Pentecostal-type revivals, so-called. The wild laughter, the falling down, the seeming comatose states that would last for hours or even days, the making of animal sounds, the trances and visions—these re-

---
26   Beardsley, 97-98.

mind me of what has been called the Laughing Revival, or the Toronto Blessing, or The River, or the Brownsville Revival—very similar behavior, with the exception of the "jerks." As to the jerks, it was reported that on some occasions the jerking was so violent that necks were broken and movement was a blur to the human eye; all these were accompanied by commotions, shouting, and screaming. Some affected by jerks continued to have those for years afterward. Yet, many looked upon the jerks as a godly manifestation; some ministers encouraged them, because the jerks, along with other excesses, seemed to draw even larger crowds.

Catharine C. Cleveland, in *The Great Revival in the West: 1797-1805,* describes the jerks in this way:

> Sometime after the beginning of the Great Revival a new exercise appeared in eastern Tennessee which came to be familiarly known as "the jerks." At first it was confined to spasmodic jerking of the forearm at short intervals; but later it affected every muscle, nerve, and tendon in the body. The "jerks" proved to be most contagious and the mere suggestion of them was sufficient to animate an entire congregation with this peculiar exercise.[27]

Sermons would be drowned out by both the exercises and by the "exhorters" who took it upon themselves to wander through the crowds calling out at the top of their lungs. The exhorters—young and old, sometimes very young and not ordained or trained ministers—shouted out encouragements to those thought to be under the influence of the Spirit. "Press into the kingdom," "repent, repent," "flee to Jesus," "Today is the day of salvation," "Trust in Jesus or burn in hell," are ex-

---

[27] Catherine C. Cleveland, The Great Revival in the West: 1797-1805 (Gloucester, MA: Peter Smith, 1959), 98-99.

amples of the messages of the exhorters. Some preachers encouraged these; others did not and considered the exhorters to be a problem. With so many thousands in attendance, and so few in authority evident, with liquor merchants setting up shop on the edges of the camps, with what became much like a country barn dance—the stage was set for various forms of immoderation.

An exercise closely associated with the jerks was "barking." The noise emitted was like a dog barking, and the jerks would often follow. Trances were experienced by many who fell to the ground, the women often having to be covered; people who remained seemingly comatose would have to be moved to the perimeter, and dancers would have to be given wide birth. Visions and prophecies were common. The aroma of perfume with a peculiar fragrance would be reported. Some would engage in a singing exercise, but the sound would not come from the throat, mouth, or nose, but from the chest. And there were other exercises as well.

Catharine Cleveland explained: "Trances and visions became common among those affected by the exercises. These in a measure fostered the prophet spirit, and many declared that the millennium was at hand."[28] Some, like Joseph Smith of the Mormons, declared that they had received revelations to the effect that they alone knew the genuine truth. Most of these prophets had little lasting influence; others struck a certain chord with people and were embraced.

The rise of Arminian theology and the decline of Calvinistic theology

It must be pointed out that "all the new sects and denominations had one thing in common—they rejected the Calvinistic understanding of the gospel that had hitherto prevailed among all evangelical Christians."[29] Though not a new sect,

---
28 Cleveland, 104.
29 Murray, 177.

the Methodists who arrived in America in 1769 called their baseline theology Arminianism. Iain H. Murray explains the difference in the theologies:

> Evangelical Arminians claimed that grace extends equally to all men and its acceptance or rejection must therefore depend ultimately on human decision. Calvinists believed that such is the ruined state of human nature that no man would respond to the gospel if repentance and faith are conditions to be fulfilled before grace renews him.[30]

The great Methodist circuit rider Francis Asbury, along with Thomas Coke, began *The Arminian Magazine* in 1789, and the opening line of the preface for the very first issue was the following:

> Brethren and Friends: We are not ignorant that the Gospel has been preached in the eastern and northern parts of these United States, from the earliest settlement of the country; but this has been done chiefly, though not entirely, through the Calvinist medium. However, in this magazine very different opinions will be defended.[31]

There was an apparent clash of theologies—a congenial clash, however, as both groups preached an orthodox gospel—but the differences were manifest also in the manner of how preaching was to be conducted and in what behavior was acceptable. In time, few preachers, regardless of denomination or theology, saw appearances of the exercises.

---
30 Ibid., 178.
31 Ibid., 179.

Meanwhile, a theology had developed to defend the exercises. Those who did the defending were known as "New Lights" and insisted that the exercises were the result of an inward light which shone into the heart as the will of God dealt individually with those who sought him. The exercises were simply not be critiqued by an appeal to Scripture, nor was common order observed.

> Those who shouted the loudest, exhorted and prayed the longest, even though this might be to the point of utter exhaustion, were considered most blessed. Disrespect for the outward form of religion was general. The young convert in lofty tone would warn sinners to fly from the wrath to come, regardless of the fact that he might be drawing the attention from the minister's sermon. In fact, services were often taken in hand by converts who considered the pulpit of little account, especially if inclined to formal sermonizing. Some would sleep through the sermon, rising to voice their own opinions the moment it was over.[32]

The excesses pose a question that may be unanswerable. Were these of a demonic nature, or were they the result of humans being out of control? Satan or bad behavior? Or was it simply frontier religion that had lost connection with biblical orderliness? The dark sides—were they sinister or silly? Maybe there is no way to be precise, but the demonic kingdom did have much to gain by both the distractions and the broadly negative tainting of the awakenings.

Barton Stone saw both extremes in the awakenings in the West. But for him, it did not mean that the whole was to be questioned:

---
32 Cleveland, 113-114.

My conviction is complete that it was a good work—the work of God; nor has my mind wavered since on the subject. Much did I see then, and much have I seen since, that I consider to be fanaticism; but this should not condemn the work. The devil has always tried to ape the works of God, to bring them into disrepute; but that cannot be a Satanic work which brings men to humble confession, to forsaking sin, to prayer, fervent praise and thanksgiving, and to a sincere and affectionate exhortation to sinner to repent and come to Jesus the Saviour.[33]

The core assumption that permitted the extremes was that the impressions, impulses, visions, dreams, prophesying, and more were an indication, even evidence, that the Holy Spirit was at work. There is almost no limit to deception once such identification is made. It was true in the first and second awakening; it was true of the Jesus People Movement. When biblically grounded ministers do take a stand against that which detracts from the gospel, such ministers may be designated as anti-revivalists or worse.

Rise of American Bible-based cults

Of most lasting negative impact on American Christianity were those who claimed new revelations. Out of the second awakening came several Bible-based cults: Mormonism, Christian Science, Jehovah's Witnesses, and the Adventist movement. It seems the more incredible the claim, the more widely it was embraced. It was akin to people having their fifteen minutes of fame. A revelation, shouted long and loud, would attract a crowd and maybe create a following. Celebrity status and a certain amount of power, however temporary, was an invigorating temptation.

---
33 Beardsley, 92.

Toward the close of the awakening there was an extraordinary interest in the Second Advent of Jesus and Millennialism, especially in the West. Jesus would return, as the Bible does teach, and then he would establish his kingdom and subdue evil—this historic pre-millennialism had been embraced periodically by Christians from the third century onward. Now however, the Baptist farmer William Miller set dates for the Second Coming, and he was not the only one to be fascinated by the subject. Then, as in more modern times, people were unusually interested in anything to do with "end time prophecy." In addition to the Adventist movement was the work of Charles Taze Russell, founder of the Jehovah's Witnesses, who also began predicting dates for Jesus' return, having been influenced by the Adventist movement. Joseph Smith and the early Mormons did not set dates for a Second Advent, but believed an "angel's" revelation to Smith of a restored Christianity that would usher in the Messianic age.

Some of the groups that were caught up in end times speculation departed from orthodox Christianity—like the Jehovah's Witnesses and Mormons—but some developed intricate scenarios of end time events while continuing to embrace normative Christian doctrines. The Plymouth Brethren in England, whose founder was John Nelson Darby, is a clear example of this. Darby's view came to be known as Dispensationalism, and primarily through the very large influence of the Schofield Study Bible, edited by C.I. Schofield and published in 1909, it came to dominate conservative, Arminian evangelicalism, especially in America.

There was also a push by some to return Christianity to a purer state. In every age it is possible to point to the deficiencies of the human organizations called churches. Thus a call to return to biblical ways will occur from within or without the broad Christian community. This is sometimes referred to as *restorationism,* the desire to restore and restructure the church. Joseph Smith of the Mormons may be viewed as a restorationist. Russell of the Jehovah's Witnesses may be so viewed. And there were others: Mary Baker Eddy of the Church of Christian Science and elements of the Adventist movement are examples. Some of these departed from orthodox Christian theology and some did not.

J. Edwin Orr, in *The Event of the Century,* now out of print but originally published by International Awakening Press, Wheaton, IL in 1989, wrote of the decline in religious life in America after the second awakening. In particular, Orr cites the confusion that resulted from the work of the Baptist farmer William Miller:

> Some people at that time lost faith in spiritual things because of the unhappy disillusionment which vexed the followers of William Miller who predicted Christ's return and reign in 1843 and 1844. The public confidence was shaken as excitement died away. A minority stood firm in their Adventist convictions, and organized to carry on a steady ministry. But some disgruntled victims swung to bitter unbelief, while others turned to a cynical materialism. So widely was the misinterpretation spread abroad that churches were subjected to derision, and faith in all religion was impaired.[34]

Impact of the second awakening

Beardsley describes three results of the second awakening: one, the overthrow of infidelity; two, the spiritual quickening of the churches; and three, the inauguration of the great philanthropic and missionary enterprises.

Churches had been in decline, practical atheism was growing, and public morality was breaking down—but this was

---
34   Orr, 7.

checked to a considerable degree as a result of the awakening. Infidels were converted to Christ, then faithfully embraced Christian doctrine and practice. Schools were established to train ministers for gospel ministry. There was the revival at Yale under Dwight, but there was also revival at Dartmouth, Williams, and other institutions.

Many churches also recovered their love for God and for each other. Many experienced a new and right spirit within them, as prayer, interest in the Scripture, and worship were again precious and sought after. New converts were gathered into the traditional denominational churches such as the Presbyterian and Congregational, but also in large numbers into the Baptist and Methodist churches, these mostly in the southern states. Many slaves were also converted, and this was to have far reaching implications as the abolition movement within the Christian denominations began to grow. Social reform and abolitionist programs were emphasized by Charles Finney, and he preached that new converts must begin immediately to work against sin. In addition to slavery, Christians concerned themselves with education, temperance, vice, world peace, women's rights, Sabbath observance, and profanity.

Slavery, and the racism that most always went with it, had been questioned by many who had been active in the first awakening. In fact, a number of slaves had been converted during that period and had become leaders in churches. Their ministry, though not always directed at the abolition of slavery, nevertheless began to stir the American conscience. During the second awakening, many slaves also were converted, and a growing attention was directed toward the immorality of slavery. Momentum in this direction built, until Christian groups like the Methodists and Baptists began to take stands against it. Gilbert H. Barnes wrote in *The Antislavery Impulse 1830-1844:*

The conjunction of so many elements of the Great Revival [1831] in the antislavery agitation was more than coincidence. In leadership, in method, and in objective, the Great Revival and the American antislavery Society now were one. It is not too much to say that for the moment the antislavery agitation as a whole was what it had long been in larger part, an aspect of the Great Revival in benevolent reform.[35]

General good came out of the awakening in the formation of various institutions like schools, missionary societies, and social organizations that served to better society as a whole. In 1810, through the efforts of Samuel J. Mills, the American Board of Commissioners for Foreign Missions began. Then the Baptist Missionary Society was begun in 1814 and the Methodist Episcopal in 1819. In addition to the foreign interest, home missions also grew. The American Home Missionary Society was founded in 1826. Bible and tract societies came into being, with the American Tract Society forming in 1814 and the American Bible Society in 1816. The American Temperance Society was founded in 1826. Colleges and seminaries to educate for the gospel ministry were founded, so that by 1827 seventeen theological seminaries had been established by various denominations.

Christian newspapers and journals sprang up as early as 1800. In 1816, the *Boston Recorder* was published by the Congregationalists, which is noted as the first weekly religious newspaper in the world. Also that year, the *Religious Intelligencer* began, then in 1819 *The Watchman* by the Baptists, in 1822 *Zion's Herald* by the Methodists, and in 1826 the Free Will Baptists came out with *The Morning Star.* This was but the beginning for Christian publishing.

---

35 From *Christian History* magazine, Vol. VIII, No. 3, Issue 23, p. 31.

Concluding remarks

One of the unintended results of the second awakening was the ascendancy of Arminian theology. By all accounts, it had won out in America over Reformed/Calvinistic theology. Charles Finney's seeming success with his popularity, notoriety, and books, especially *Revival Lectures,* insured that future evangelists would adopt his strategy, the kernel of which had been established by Timothy Dwight in the early 1800s with the concept that revival could be initiated by human effort. Finney fleshed out this notion in actual evangelistic practice and ritualized it to a degree, so that his example has been followed by nearly every evangelist since. The "old measures" of Asahel Nettleton and those like him, especially the great preachers of the first awakening in America—Edwards, Whitefield, the Tennents, Dickinson, Blair, Davies, and so many more—were brushed aside and virtually lost. These evangelists did pray, plan, and preach for revival but were biblically pentecostal, in that they would leave the saving activity to the Holy Spirit. The "old measures" consisted of only the proclamation of the gospel message of the person and work of Jesus Christ. Now, however, revival and evangelism were increasingly considered to be in the hands of people and no longer exclusively the work of a sovereign God. Despite this large paradigm shift, God was about to bring a third awakening to America, and it would prove to be quite unlike anything that had gone before.

Three:
The Third Awakening in America (a.1857 - a.1859)

Dates

Fixing the dates of awakenings is elusive if not impossible. As we have observed in the two earlier American awakenings, we again have this difficulty with the beginning for the third awakening, though historians have fairly well settled on 1857; of course there are some who will point to "times of refreshing" that preceded 1857. Figuring into this uncertainty is the ministry of Phoebe Palmer, whose preaching had notable success years prior to the general time given for the commencement of the third awakening.

1858 is the usual date for the ending of the third awakening, but after consulting J. Edwin Orr's *The Event of the Century*, I am inclined to point to 1859 as the end date, since it took some time for the revival to reach the Deep South. However, the general consensus is that the third awakening "crested" in mid-1858.

Compounding the ending date problem is what to do with the awakening that occurred amidst the Northern and Southern armies during the Civil War, which, by all accounts, was significant and even dramatic. It is thought that 21% of the Army of the Confederacy was converted by war's end. Was this awesome outpouring an extension of the third awakening or something new and separate? While some claim one thing and others another, my view is that it is impossible to know.

Perhaps the determining factors in fixing dates are estimates of the growth in church membership and baptisms. This is more nearly possible for the third awakening than any other, because there is a plethora of data to examine. Here is a summary of J. Edwin Orr's estimations: Protestant denominations dividing into nineteen or twenty-two categories show that in 1857-58 there were 478,514 additions and in 1858-59 there were 565,367 additions to membership. Before 1857 and after 1860 the number of additions is far less.[36] Thus, it may be legitimate to fix dates based on statistics.[37]

The difference between normal and awakening times may play a role. As stated before, during normal times there will be additions, but the numbers of conversions, baptisms, and growth in church membership sharply go up in times of awakening.

Historians examining the first and second awakenings have noted significant increases in some statistics that point to growth beyond what is normal. Statistical measurements for key data that clearly reveals the third awakening to have been remarkable also help define the dates. The fourth awakening—the Jesus People Movement of the late 1960s and early 1970s—lack, at least in this point in time, reliable statistics to clearly mark beginning and ending dates.

Distinguishing characteristics of awakenings

Preaching of the gospel in established New England churches was the most dominant characteristic of the first awakening. That era was known for its great preachers—Theodore Jacob Frelinghuysen, George Whitefield, Jonathan Edwards, Gilbert Tennent, Samuel Davies, Jonathan Dickinson, and a host of others.

---

36   Orr, *The Event of the Century*, 327.
37   Note: the population of America in 1857 was about 30,000,000.

THE THIRD AWAKENING IN AMERICA (A.1857 - A.1859)

The first part of the second awakening was much the same as the first awakening—preaching of the gospel in established churches and educational institutions, with Timothy Dwight at Yale and Asahel Nettleton being two of the most outstanding preachers. This was the case in New England, while in the west, there were the camp meetings with their focus on communion. James McGready, Peter Cartwright, Barton Stone, along with a host of other preachers from the Presbyterians, Methodists, and Baptists denominations led the revival. Charles Finney, in the second phase of the second awakening, was also a preacher and evangelist, but there was a difference with Finney and those who followed him: there was a dependence upon the decision capacity of the individual with means developed to facilitate this.

In the third awakening, prayer meetings were the focal point, led for the most part by non-professional lay people, especially in the early part of the awakening. As time went on, the awakening came to be dominated by fewer lay people as traveling evangelists began to dominate the scene.

In the fourth awakening—the Jesus People Movement—the gospel was again central, but it was not centered in churches, in communion services, or in prayer meetings. Then the gospel was presented primarily through personal testimony or witness, and the audience was mostly teenagers and young adults. This was at least true earlier in the awakening. However, by 1970 all the standard forms of American-style evangelism were being employed—music, films, large meetings, advertising, slick publications, and so on.

Between the second and third awakening

The age of the traveling evangelist had dawned with Charles G. Finney's success in the 1820s and 1830s. Newspapers and magazines reported on the large numbers of people being counted as converts at Finney meetings. By 1840, infatuation with head-count statistics played no small part in the rapid growth in the numbers of professional evangelists. Most of the major denominations had their specialists. Indeed, competition for numbers began to rule. However, a focus on growth was accompanied by a general decline in morality and genuine spirituality.

One of the reasons for the decline was spiritual confusion, especially in regard to receiving what were thought to be messages, impressions, and prophesies from God—these had been characteristic of the second awakening as it was experienced in the West. One instance in particular proved to have a profound impact on the American public—William Miller and the subsequent Adventist movement. Miller, an evangelist and self-proclaimed prophet, was a Baptist farmer turned restorationist (like Joseph Smith of the Mormons). Miller forecast that Jesus would return on March 21, 1843. When that failed, Miller revised his prediction to March 21, 1844, then October 22, 1844. Each time, the faithful made life changing preparations for the expected second advent and then gathered on hillsides dressed in special robes to await the return of Jesus. The media loved it, reported it, and mocked it, and the result was a general spiritual and religious depression that touched all of America.

In October 1857 there was a financial panic that gripped America for a relatively short period of time. Some commentators were convinced that the economic distress was the immediate cause of the third awakening, explaining that money trouble drove people to their knees in prayer and was the explanation for the phenomenon that was to follow.

J. Edwin Orr argues strongly against the concept of a "bank-panic revival." Orr quotes Talbot W. Chambers, a Dutch Reformed minister:

> But does adversity always lead men to God? In the year 1837, there happened a commercial revulsion, quite as widespread and as unex-

pected as that of 1857 and tenfold more disastrous; yet there was then no unusual turning to religion, no mighty movement of the popular mind, and no up-heaving of the foundations. People were far more intent upon examining the political and economic causes than its spiritual bearings.[38]

The Wall Street crash of 1929 did not result in a mass turning to God and religion, and Orr quotes an economist, Roger Babson: "there has been no significant correlation between periods of depression and periods of revival in the United States."[39] To illustrate this, it can also be pointed out that the prayer meetings in New York, Boston, and Philadelphia were begun before the panic of October 1857 commenced.

Canadian awakenings and the Palmers

In October of 1857, particularly in Ontario and Quebec, Canada, there were "harvests" in the camp meetings that Walter and Phoebe Palmer conducted. At the McNab Street Wesleyan Church in Hamilton, Ontario, the preaching of the Palmers saw 600 people make professions of faith in Christ; many commentators conclude that this is an indicator that the awakening was *on*.

Phoebe Palmer emerged as the leading preacher of the two, and her ministry saw a continuing number of conversions. It should be noted that the Palmers operated in the fashion developed and popularized by Charles Finney, especially making use of the altar call, which made it possible for the counting of the "converted."

Whether the Palmers used the format of the camp meeting, as they did early in their ministry, or preached in established churches, the meetings were decent and in order. But

---

38   Ibid., 20.
39   Ibid.

at around the very same period in New York City, something entirely new was about to begin.

The noon businessman's prayer meeting

> The Old Dutch North Church at Fulton and Williams streets in New York City had a decision to make. The church had fallen on hard times. Many families had moved out of the metropolis to safer and more pleasant communities. The neighborhood was being taken over by a floating population seeking jobs in the businesses which surrounded the church. Migrant laborers flooded the area—with everything in mind except going to an evangelical church to hear the gospel. Most of the community expected the Old Dutch church to follow suit.[40]

On September 23, 1857, three weeks before the financial panic, Jeremiah Lamphier, a forty-six year old businessman, began a noon hour prayer meeting for men like himself. He had been converted in 1842 at the Broadway Tabernacle in New York City, a church founded by Charles Finney in 1836. He had been hired by the North Dutch Reformed Church as an urban evangelist, in hopes that the church might be able to grow and thus stay and minister on Fulton Street. This came after efforts at visitation and other forms of evangelism seemed to bring no results. Initially, Lamphier planned for only a weekly prayer meeting, and the meetings progressed on this schedule slowly in the beginning; but later it became necessary to meet daily. September 23, 1857 was the date of that first prayer meeting.[41]

---

40 John Thornbury, "The 1857 National Revival USA" (*Evangelical Times*, Darlington, UK), September 2007
41 Wesley Duewal's *Revival Fire* beautifully describes the ministry of Lamphier. Published in 1995 by Zondervan Publishing House.

The financial panic of 1857 followed closely on the heels of the earliest prayer meetings on Fulton Street and likely helped attendance at first, but the panic, as discussed above, was not the real reason for the awakening. Certainly, a sovereign God can use circumstances for his own purpose, but the panic was not long in duration, ending December 15, whereas the awakening lasted at least two more years.

From New York, the prayer meeting format spread to Philadelphia, Boston, and finally to nearly every major city in America, and not merely major cities, but also to a vast majority of America's small towns and villages. This point cannot be overstated.

It is not to be assumed that the Fulton Street prayer meeting founded by Jeremiah Lamphier either caused or marked the beginning of the third awakening, and the same must be said of the ministry of the Palmers. This is nearly impossible to document, but it appears very probable that what Lamphier was doing in New York was going on at the same time in other places as well—not the exact format Lamphier eventually adopted, but there were also meetings for prayer springing up in places across America. To be clearer: there was no "fountain head" of the third awakening. It did not necessarily begin in New York and spread from there. As in the Jesus People Movement, what began perhaps in San Francisco in 1967 did not spread throughout the country as leaven moves through dough, but rather the same forms appeared in many places at once—without human intent nor intervention nor requiring a long period of time. This is one mark of a genuine awakening and thus not the product of human engineering.

Across the country the prayer meetings generally copied the format set by Lamphier in New York. *Christian History* provides the following description of the prayer meeting:

> The form of worship was always the same: any person might pray, give a testimony or an

exhortation, or lead in singing as he or she "felt led." Although pastors such as [Henry Ward] Beecher often attended and lent their enthusiastic support, lay-people provided the leadership. Little planning was done for the meetings; the chief rules were that a meeting should begin punctually, and no one should speak or pray for very long.[42]

J. Edwin Orr describes the prayer meetings:

> This mode of worship was adopted in all the meetings. There was no order of service, no prepared plan. Any person attending might pray, or exhort, or lead in song, or give a testimony, as he felt moved, the only restriction being the five-minute time limit, and the only prohibition any controversial subject such as slavery or baptism, both subject to the bell. Distinction of denomination was ignored and any preferment of ministers over laymen disregarded. The informal freedom of rural camp meetings was thus transferred to the urban auditorium in the busy downtown city.[43]

Conduct for the prayer meetings were written up and a copy would be given to each prayer meeting leader.[44] Orr, in the same volume quoted above, gives a sample of the written instructions:

---

42   A. K. Curtis and Keith J. Hardman, eds., "The Time for Prayer: The Third Great Awakening" (*Christian History*, Volume VIII, No. 3 Issue 23), 33.
43   Orr, 288.
44   Note: an actual hand bell would be rung to signal a subject that was considered out of order. Very effective! Also, it has been suggested that the founders of Alcoholic Anonymous borrowed from the prayer meeting format for their meetings. Indeed, there is some resemblance.

Be prompt, commencing precisely at twelve o'clock. The Leader is not expected to exceed ten minutes in opening up the meeting.

1st   Open the meeting by singing of from three to five verses of a hymn.

2nd   Offer prayer.

3rd   Read a portion of the Scripture.

4th   Say that the meeting is now open for prayers and exhortations, observing particularly the rules overhead, and inviting the brethren from abroad to take part in the service.

5th   Read but one or two requests at a time, requiring a prayer to follow, such prayer to have special reference to the same.

6th   In case of any suggestion or any proposition by any person, say this is simply a prayer-meeting, and that they are out of order, and call on some brother to pray.

7th   Give out the closing hymn at five minutes before one o'clock. Request the benediction from a clergyman, if one be present.[45]

Men made up the vast majority of those attending the prayer meetings, though as the awakening progressed, women began to appear. Often attendees submitted written prayer requests to the "desk," which would sometimes be read by the

---

45   Ibid., 282.

leader to the gathering, given time restraints, and someone would be asked to offer up a prayer with that request in mind. Confessions of sin—sincere, straight-forward, and humble confessions—were made.

There were testimonies, often containing significant gospel content, and there were "exhorters," meaning that lay people would preach short messages, usually of a gospel nature, but not to exceed the five minute time limit. This continued throughout the awakening with more and more exhorting as time went by.

People could come and go as they pleased. In crowded, popular meetings, some people would spend only a few minutes in the meeting and leave for someone else to take their places.

Charismatic gifts were not in evidence—no speaking in tongues, prophecy, revelations, nor visions—as might be associated with Pentecostalism. The singing could be grand and soulful; indeed, many of the finest hymns in our hymnbooks were written and became popular during the third awakening. Mostly, the singing was without musical accompaniment, and there were no choirs.

To copy the format of the prayer meetings of the third awakening would not guarantee an awakening would follow. It must be thoroughly grasped that no two awakenings are alike and that God will do what he will do. Additionally, an awakening does not progress without the preaching of the gospel in some manner or another. Faith always comes by hearing and hearing by the preaching of Christ (see Romans 10:17). There was much praying, and there was much preaching, but the preaching was not the same as in the first and second awakenings. The Jesus People Movement was unlike any of the previous three American awakenings. Still, when God does bring awakening, it is the word of Jesus and the cross that will be the fundamental "means."

Widespread support for the awakening

The third awakening was widely reported by the newspapers: it was front-page news. The first two awakenings had many detractors, both within and without the Christian community. Both of these earlier awakenings had their obvious down sides, which were plainly visible to the watching world. This was especially true of the second awakening. However, the third awakening was different. Orr writes:

> A remarkable feature of the 1857-58 Revival in North America was the almost unanimous approval that it received. It was indeed difficult to find someone with unkind words to offer. Critics were unable to lay the charges of fanaticism, or hysteria, or any of the usual accusations against revivals. As Bishop McIlvaine affirmed, it was reputable, commanding in unusual ways the world's respect. It received cordial commendation from the President, governors, majors, members of the professions, businessmen, universities and colleges. It was said that it was so obviously of God that men seemed almost afraid to be critical of it.[46]

Orr's Characteristics of the awakening

Following are a number of characteristics of the third awakening as described by Orr; among them I make some brief comments:

One: "Not the work of a famous man. The awakening of 1858 had no recognized leader or leaders. It was no man's monument."

---
46   Ibid., 239.

Two: "The leadership of laymen. This outpouring of the Holy Spirit removed the shyness and embarrassment of laymen in general and of businessmen in particular."

I am among those who do not like to make a large distinction between "professional" and "lay" Christians, while recognizing that God will gift who and how he will. However, at that time the difference between the ordained and trained clergy and others in the church was notable. It was during this awakening that the forms most used in the awakening—praying, exhorting, the giving of testimonies of conversion, and music, in fact large amounts of music toward the ending of the awakening—could be brought forth by anyone.

Three: "The use of means."

Certain means, or techniques, or methods were used, but they were of the ordinary kind—prayer and the proclamation of the Word. Means had been used in the second awakening, especially through the ministry of Charles Finney—the large city gatherings, the anxious bench, the altar call, and other processes designed to register decisions—but here there were no unusual means. The awakening was not humanly engineered. It began suddenly and unexpectedly and ended in the same manner, despite what people would have done.

Four: "Emotional extravagance. The 1857-58 Awakening differed from earlier awakenings before and after 1800. The work was singularly free from the emotionalism which accompanied earlier movements." Orr went on to say, *"Neither in 1857, nor in 1858, nor later, was there outbreaking of trembling, jerking, screaming, groaning, fainting, prostration, or dancing for joy."*

Five: "Gifts of the Spirit. In light of manifestations in the Pentecostal movement following 1906 and in the Charismatic movement half a century later, it must be noted that records of the 1858 Revival present no evidence of glossolalia, its interpretation, healing, or other signs and wonders."

Six: "Christian Fraternity. The Great Awakening of 1857-58 produced the highest degree of real cooperation and unity among the various evangelical Christian denominations until then known in modern times." Orr goes on to make the point even clearer. "So striking was this manifestation of Christian love that it was regarded by various contemporary observers as the most significant characteristic of the revival."

No one denomination was specially blessed by the awakening. To one degree or another, evangelical churches benefited, even those who kept their distance. Some who were reluctant to authenticate the awakening benefited from it in the way of membership growth and baptisms. It did not matter whether the theology was Arminian or Calvinistic, as long as there was prayer and preaching.

The usual lines were drawn, however, between leaders of liberal and non-Christian groups and those who embraced the awakening. Even here some appreciation and approval was demonstrated by non-evangelicals. The awakening was not easily criticized.

The awakening's impact on Jews

"One of the most unusual characteristics of the 1857-58 Revival was its powerfully persuasive influence upon the Jews, so many of whom participated in the operations of the New York movement."[47]

In New York, mostly centered in Brooklyn, the Jewish population numbered around 35,000. Jews would have been able to observe first hand much of the impact of the noon hour prayer meetings that eventually covered the city. Some Jewish leaders were closed to it, others were neutral, and others endorsed it, especially as they saw the numbers turning to prayer. It was one rabbi's opinion that Jews ought to pray like the Christians.

---
47   Ibid., 246.

It is not known how many Jewish people embraced Jesus as their Messiah at this point in time, but estimates put it at several dozen at least.

Dark side of the awakening

The third awakening was nearly forgotten by historians, despite the fact that nearly the whole of America was touched by it and that more than one out of every thirty Americas were converted during its short span. A number of reasons are given for this forgetfulness. One, it was of a shorter duration than other awakenings—two or three years, and it began to fade away. Two, the Civil War, which followed on its heels, quickly overshadowed all else. Three, there was almost no downside to the awakening— neither scandals nor strange phenomena, neither cultic nor sectarian groups rising up out of it to attract media attention. Four, the Christian community generally, with some exceptions, united behind the awakening, so that there was a minimum of debate and argument; fights would have attracted attention. Five, there was no outstanding preacher or evangelist; rather there were hundreds, even thousands, of preachers and exhorters whom God equipped and empowered for short durations. Leaders of earlier American awakenings—like Jonathan Edwards, George Whitefield, James McGready, Peter Cartwright, Asahel Nettleton, Charles Finney, and many others—continued their ministries over the course of many years, and their names became associated with the might works of God, with the media of the time focused on the big names and the details of their ministries. This awakening was not glamorous.

American Christians took notice, however, as there had never been a time in their history when so many persons were added to church membership. The awakening numbers seemed to exceed, proportionately, those of even the first awakening, the great Pentecost we read about in the Book of Acts.

The awakening and the Abolition Movement

For many decades prior to the onset of the third awakening consciences were being stirred by slavery and the racism that accompanied it. Christians were often at the forefront of the national controversy, and it weighed heavily upon many. Christians, both north and south, began to speak out on the issue, and sides were taken. The Methodists confronted the issue so strongly that there was a major shakeup among them. In 1845, the Baptists literally split in two over slavery. All Christian denominations became embroiled to one degree or another. And yes, southern preachers used the Bible to defend slavery; some of these defended it on political grounds—states' rights versus federal control.

It is arguable that the second and third awakenings did more than anything else in the American experience to produce a climate of intolerance to slavery. Slavery was preached as an evil like no other, and many a convert of the awakenings sought to end the institution. The third awakening, coming when it did, may have been that moral empowering to finally confront great national sin, come what may.

The awakening and the Civil War

The awakening did not prevent the war. Does that fact flaw its credibility or power? Were so many converted because so very many would die? These questions must be left for others to answer; I bring them up here because they will linger in the minds of many.

A sovereign God knows the future from the beginning—this is a biblically accurate conclusion. Could not God then intervene in another way, one that is less horrific than a war with hundreds of thousands of casualties? We will ask such questions and not likely find satisfying answers. What is clear is that in the third American awakening God poured out his Spirit in a manner and magnitude unprecedented in American history.

Four:
The Fourth Awakening in America? The Jesus People Movement (a.1967 - a.1972)

Unlike the generalized approach used for the first three awakenings, this chapter on the Jesus People Movement (from now on referred to as the JPM) will be intentionally autobiographical. During most of the years of the JPM, I kept a journal, wrote newsletters, and took pictures. Over the years I drew up a history or two of the period and preached several sermons with the JPM as a back drop. Now I hope to bring all this together to give one participant's account of what may have been America's fourth or, maybe, fifth awakening.

The most complete history of the movement to date has been written by Larry Eskridge as a doctoral dissertation, and I will not attempt to duplicate his fine work. His will be titled: *God's Forever Family: The Jesus People Movement in America*

Dates for the Jesus People Movement (a. 1967-a.1972)

In common with the other great awakenings in America, the dates above are approximate; some historians lump the Jesus People Movement with the 1950s healing movement, the Catholic Renewal that followed Vatican II, and the more general ecumenical charismatic movement that seemed to spring up about the same time as the JPM. (I was a part, to some degree, of each of these except the 1950s healing movement.) Here the JPM will be treated as something that stands alone, though the JPM may have been impacted by each of the other movements.[48]

If the JPM, the Catholic Renewal and the Charismatic Movement are to be connected, the date for what I will call America's fourth awakening should be moved backward to 1964 or even earlier. My own involvement began in February of 1967.

The ending date of the JPM, according to my own experience in California's San Francisco Bay Area, came in 1972. A number of my contemporaries think 1975 is a more accurate date. Indeed, some think it is still going on today but is now called by different names.

"Movement"

Those who were involved in the JPM did not name it. At some point after 1970 the term began to appear in print. It was news to us that we were part of a movement, and at first we did not readily accept the designation. Typically, we called ourselves "street Christians," since our ministry and lives were not centered in churches. Our work was on the street, with personal evangelism being the major activity—at least in the beginning.

"Jesus People"—a term applied by the media—became acceptable to us. Before that, and alongside it, was "Jesus Freak." There were times when I used this last term to describe myself. It does not sound very flattering today, but in those days I did not experience it as a demeaning term.

It was not until the 1990s that it came to my attention that I had been a part of something unusual. My conversion had occurred in 1963, so the JPM was only a few years removed from my new birth, affording me little time to gain an understanding of what an awakening was. I knew what the term

---
48   See Appendix B

"revival" meant, since putting on revivals was a normal part of my being a pastor of a small country Southern Baptist church. But what we were doing in San Francisco's Haight-Ashbury I would not have called a revival. Doing personal evangelism on the street was simply ordinary and practical ministry for the circumstances of the time and place.

Earlier movements

It was not until 1968 that I became acquainted with the Charismatic Movement, mainly the Catholic version of it. It was a year later at Holy Innocents Episcopal Church in Corte Madera, California, that I connected with the Charismatic Movement. Father Todd Ewald began bringing a fellow Episcopalian priest, Father Dennis Bennett of Seattle, Washington, to preach and minister at Holy Innocents around that time, and many of the Jesus People started attending. I recall an elderly lady named Gert Bohanna who often ministered there. The services were fairly charismatic but not wildly so, and while there was healing and speaking in tongues, the main focus was on preaching the gospel and teaching the Bible. Wherever Jesus was preached and the Bible taught, Jesus People would show up.

We learned from the teachers and preachers of the Charismatic Movement, especially from the Ft. Lauderdale Five, as we called them—Bob Mumford, Charles Simpson, Derek Prince, Don Basham, and Ern Baxter. These men were older than most of the Jesus People and were experienced, mature Christians. The dozens of teaching tapes they produced we eagerly sought out and listened to for hours and hours. If we heard that one of these men was to be preaching anywhere near us, we were there. Mainline Pentecostals like Oral Roberts and Kathryan Kuhlman were also of interest as were several other preachers and teachers who caught our attention—names that escape me now.

Jesus People, though influenced by charismatics and pentecostals, were nevertheless distinct from these, at least in the earliest years. The same is true of the Catholic renewal or the Catholic version of the Charismatic Movement—at least according to my experience—but I think it is generally accurate of the entire JPM. As to the origin of the charismatic and Catholic Renewal movements—my guess is that they preceded the JPM. They may have been a part of the awakening, but my experience tells me they were not related.

There was a Marist seminary in San Rafael, where I was living from late 1968 until 1985, and one or two of their priests/monks visited the Bible studies we conducted. In time, I was invited to their masses and occasionally participated in these. There was also a Carmelite Monastery in San Rafael offering a public prayer service that was widely attended by Jesus People and charismatics from a number of different churches. Still, the JPM was different and distinct from the Catholic charismatic expression, though many people moved freely between these.

Pentecostalism was something I resisted early on, but my stance gradually softened. The avoidance had originated shortly after my conversion when I was given a book on the American-based Bible cults—Mormons, Jehovah Witnesses, Christian Science, Adventism, and *Pentecostalism*. This book would probably not be published now, because Adventists and pentecostals have basically moved into the mainstream, but up until the charismatic movement became widespread, the insistence by most pentecostals that speaking in tongues was not only the evidence of Holy Spirit Baptism but of conversion itself created a negative attitude among Baptists like myself. However, in the early years of the JPM, it was often the charismatic and pentecostal churches of whatever denomination that opened their doors to Jesus People. Thus, the Jesus People were a mixed bag theologically and experientially. For the most part, I retained my Baptistic theology but adopted charismatic expressions such as an emphasis on speaking in tongues, healing, and predictive forms of prophecy.

How it all began for me

In 1955, just before I turned thirteen, my parents moved from my birthplace of Portland, Oregon, to Sunland-Tujunga, smallish twin towns in the northern end of Los Angeles snuggled up against the San Gabriel Mountains. It was a short drive to Hollywood, and under the influence of Jack Kerouac's *On the Road,* I became a wannabe beatnik and started going to beat hangouts. Chief among these were Cosmo Alley, just off Hollywood Boulevard, and Pandora's Box out on Sunset Strip. I had gone from being a Southern California surfer dude to a dharma bum—a short trip. It was in this period that I became attracted to alternative life styles, so when the hippie thing happened in San Francisco, I both knew what it was about and identified with it.

By the time I was nineteen years old, I was married and a member of the United States Air Force. (This was not unusual at that time in history.) At Travis Air Force Base in Fairfield, California, I worked as a medic with 2nd Casualty Staging Flight. The year was 1963, and due to the urging of my wife Bobbie (Roberta Davidson), we attended a local church—First Baptist Church of Fairfield, California, where Bob Lewis was the pastor. After a few weeks, I found myself one Sunday morning at the end of Pastor Lewis' sermon trying to prevent my wife from "walking the aisle," but ending up in the middle of the aisle under many staring eyes, I made the best of my discomfort by joining her up front. I prayed the traditional sinner's prayer with Deacon Al Becker, and on the promise of my baptism, I became a member of a Southern Baptist Church.

Nothing changed for me, because I was still the same old Kent I had always been. However, I was now stuck in a commitment to attend church from time to time, if not regularly. And every time I did and had to listen to Pastor Lewis preach,

I felt worse and worse. Of course, I knew I was not a Christian and tended to consider the whole thing as a joke, but it began to wear on me. Though I was an average sinner—nothing special or extreme—I had a sense of being lost, accompanied by a growing fear of judgment. For some months this unpleasant kind of dread persisted then gave way to thinking about Jesus and what he was all about. I began to listen more carefully to the sermons. Some of my Christian friends at the Travis Air Force Base Hospital, among whom were Vern Hogue and Don Etheridge, talked with me. I still could not make any sense of the Bible and could not pick it up and read it. Then, just before my baptism (it was nine months between my coming forward and the baptism, due to a new building being built and Pastor Lewis' desire to make a big splash at the new building's dedication), I understood that Jesus was the savior. Two things I had now learned: One, I was a sinner, and two, Jesus was the savior. That must have been about the time of my conversion, but it is impossible for me to know exactly the where, when, and how of that conversion.

My new birth was evidenced by the fact that now I loved the Bible, even found time to pray, and was at the First Baptist Church of Fairfield every time I could. Pastor Bob Lewis went from being a rube from Arkansas to being a great man of God.

There was a point, some two years later, where I felt a calling to go into the ministry. My church licensed me and affirmed my call. Immediately, I informed the head of the psychology department at Sacramento State University, where I was in a master's program in counseling, that I was leaving for seminary training. In August of 1965 I was settling into life at a Southern Baptist school, Golden Gate Baptist Theological Seminary in Mill Valley, California.

The professor of missions and evangelism at Golden Gate was Dr. Francis DuBose. His passion for the gospel had a great impact on me. For weeks at a time he would preach/teach on Jesus' statement found in John 20:21, "As the Father has sent me, even so I am sending you." He stoked the fire I already had in me to be a witness for Christ. He remained a wonderful friend and encourager during the days of the JPM and afterward. It was Dr. DuBose who would later on bring me to Lincoln Park Baptist Church in San Francisco's Richmond District, from where our very first Christian house would be launched, named Soul Inn.

Without the GI Bill I might not have survived financially at the seminary. Bobbie worked at a drug store and later for the phone company; I sold shoes at J.C. Penney, was a psych technician at a local hospital, and then became pastor of a SBC church, Excelsior Baptist Church in Byron, California, in 1966, and remained there as a bi-vocational pastor for two and a half years.

One cold, rainy night in February, 1967, I was driving my 1956 black and white Ford south on Highway 101 very near the exit for Golden Gate Seminary. Bobbie and I lived on campus with our two young daughters, Dory and Grace. It was my second year in the MDiv degree program, and I was pastoring the little church on weekends. I was listening to a popular rock station, KFRC, and Scott McKenzie's hit song with the words, *"When you come to San Francisco be sure to wear a flower in your hair"* was playing. Right in the middle of that song it was as though I heard God telling me to go to the hippies in San Francisco. It may be that it was not God at all but that I was talking to myself. Who knows these things, and I make no claim one way or the other. However, the very next night about eight o'clock I drove into the city, found the Haight-Ashbury District, and started walking around.

At that point I didn't look much like a hippie, but I did have my military boots and field jacket on. People I ran into may have thought I was a deserter or AWOL. It was cold and drizzly, and after having exhausted what was to be seen on Haight Street, I wandered one block back of Haight Street to Waller Street, found a Methodist Church (which is still there and functioning), and stood on the street staring through a window. A young hippie came up to me while I was gazing into the activities in the church and struck up a conversation with me. He asked me if I wanted to learn about real religion, and I said I would. In response then he walked me a block or more away to the door of a large Victorian type house. He wanted me to meet David Hoyt, who was a person of note in the Haight. He was one of four members of the upcoming "Summer of Love" and a chief devotee at the Hare Krishna Temple on Fredrick Street, a few blocks away and near Kezar Stadium, home to the Forty-niners pro football team.

David Hoyt, recently paroled from Lompoc Federal Penitentiary, had been a jail house guru of sorts and was living in a utility closet under the grand staircase of the Victorian. He was the lone male in the house, a token, since all other members of the household were lesbians. David greeted me cordially, and we spent two or more hours talking about religion. I knew next to nothing about Hinduism and absolutely nothing about Swami Bhaktivedanta and the International Society for Krishna Consciousness. David knew something of the Bible and Christianity, but not much, so we had a lot to talk about, and we did this for weeks, hours at a time. After a couple of months, David moved into the basement of the Hare Krishna Temple and he invited me to move our chats there, which were now turning into Bible studies. At this point, I had an interview with the Swami, since he had to approve my presence at the temple. He agreed to the study but with the stipulation that I had to sit through their "kirtans," or worship services, which consisted of three chants, each lasting about one half hour. Spiritual battle ensued, and I often struggled against the sense of being compelled to join in the chanting and embrace Krishna Consciousness.

A fellow student at Golden Gate was Timothy Wu, from Taiwan I believe, who had impressed me with his deep dedication to Christ. We shared a love of personal evangelism, so

I invited him to come with me to one of the Bible studies at the temple. Timothy quickly agreed, and at the conclusion of the one study he did attend he approached David and told him that God would bring him out of that temple within three weeks. I can see the two of them now—a confrontation, and carried on with some heat.

Some weeks later, David called me one Saturday morning, very excited, asking me to rush down to the temple. When I arrived, smoke was still rolling out the front door, a fire truck was parked outside, and hoses were strewn everywhere. On the walls of the temple David (I learned later) had written in large letters Christian slogans such as "Jesus is Lord." The scene inside the temple was chaotic and confused, but I found David hurrying to rescue some of his belongings from the basement. Apparently, the Hindu altar he had built down there had mysteriously burst into flames. David and I left as quickly as possible, but not before a few members of the temple attacked me and tried to choke me to death. A fireman saw my ordeal and rescued me. Then David rode with me to the seminary and moved in with my family there.

David's appearance was a combination of hippie and eastern religious devotee; nevertheless he strolled around the campus and even sat in on classes. Students and teachers alike were welcoming and friendly. My family adapted quickly, too. During those winter days in the apartment, David and I engaged in long theological and biblical conversations, almost discipleship 101.

After a couple of weeks, when David had grasped some of the Christian basics, we began regular forays into the City to witness to the hippies in the Haight.

What we experienced

For three and a half years I was involved in street witnessing in the Haight-Ashbury, mostly along the sunny side of Haight Street from Masonic to Stanyan and on into Golden

Gate Park and Hippie Hill. During this time I had no idea that there was an awakening going on. I thought it was the way followers of Jesus normally carried on.

Direct, personal evangelism was our primary form of ministry. My favorite targets were kids carrying sleeping bags sitting on steps of the houses in the area or on the curbs. They, like me, had heard McKenzie's song but had found their way to San Francisco to get in on the dope and the sex and the fun of it all. The fun ran out in the summer of 1968 (which is another story) when the Haight turned into a hell hole. Despite it all, many youngsters from all over America turned to Christ; many of these were sent back to their parents, but some stayed and carried on with the work of the Spirit. There were dramatic conversions, often without much of a witness being given at all. One hippie, after hearing only one word spoken, simply fell to his knees in the middle of the side walk and started praying loudly to Jesus. This would happen on the street, in stores, on Hippie Hill, or on the way to that place, and crowds would sometimes gather to listen to our preaching. We handed out thousands of homemade flyers or tracts. I wrote the text usually, David did the art work, and friendly churches would sometimes do the printing. We had little or no money, no support, and no church to back us, at least for the first year or so.

Up through 1968 I was still pastor of Excelsior Baptist Church in Byron. David occasionally joined me in Byron, especially working with Hispanic migrant workers. While in prison, David had "run" with Mexicans and so could communicate with them.

After a time the church building was packed out with the workers and their families; but trouble soon came our way from the Catholic Church in Brentwood, a nearby town, as two German Shepherds were turned lose on us and our church building was vandalized. The deacons were understandably upset.

Joe Smith was the Southern Baptist area missionary for East Contra Costa County, and the church in Byron was under his supervision. He supported and encouraged me in ways I did not recognize then. I will never forget the day Joe came along with Dr. DuBose and visited me and my family at Golden Gate Seminary, bringing us bags of groceries and an envelope filled with cash.

By 1968 others also began to make the Haight a mission field. I recall that Dick Key opened up Clayton House, a block above Haight Street, from which Dick and others from the Assembly of God denomination tried to evangelize. Then Ted Wise, Danny Sands, Rick Sacks, Steve Heathner, Jim Dopp, and Lonnie Frisbee opened up in a store front on Page Street a ministry they called The Living Room. This outreach was sponsored and supported by John Streeter and Howard Day of First Baptist Church of San Francisco, Ed Plowman of Presidio Baptist Church in San Francisco, John McDonald, who was then pastor of the First Baptist Church of Mill Valley—all of these American Baptist congregations—and a number of others. (To this last church, Mill Valley, I was called as pastor in 1985 and have been pastor ever since. It is now called Miller Avenue Baptist Church.)

Sometime in 1968 I was asked to join with these men in the organization Evangelical Concerns. And in late 1968 I had the pleasure of bringing to that fine group of missionary-minded, older statesmen, Francis DuBose, then professor of missions and evangelism at Golden Gate Seminary, and Martin (later Moishe) Rosen, who would later found the missionary organization Jews for Jesus in 1973.

The Anchor Rescue Mission

David had met two middle-aged African American ladies who operated a rescue mission in the Fillmore District, which bordered the Haight. David would visit the mission to get food, but would stay at the ladies' request and preach to the hippie kids who made the relatively short trek from the Haight to the mission. Eventually, we both landed there—peeling potatoes, cooking, cleaning up, preaching, and teaching. One day one of the ladies, Sister Yvonne, told me that a man who was a regular visitor to the mission had demon problems. Up until then, I doubted the existence of a personal devil and completely dismissed the idea of demons. This was due, no doubt, to my exposure to university-oriented psychology prevalent at the time. Late one night, after all the dishes were done, the hippies who stayed to talk had been counseled, and the ladies had gone home, I was sitting by a space heater thinking about getting to bed (I would periodically stay overnight at the mission), when the person who was suspected of having demons suddenly emerged from the back of the kitchen and began to make the rather long walk toward the front door. Ah, I thought, now to test this demon business. As I spoke aloud the word, "Jesus," the subject jumped straight up in the air. I tried this about four or five times, and he responded in the same manner without ever looking at me. Following that, I began to rethink my theology, and from that point on, the casting out of demons became a regular, even normal part of the ministry in which I was engaged. This is not to say that casting out of demons was common to the JPM as a whole; in fact, some groups took decided stands against it.

Our first Christian houses

Late in 1968 the Philpott family moved from 10A Judson Lane at Golden Gate Seminary, with David Hoyt and his wife Victoria, to San Rafael to a rental on D Street. This was the beginning of a Christian commune called Zion's Inn. Earlier that year, Al Gossett, the pastor of Lincoln Park Baptist Church and a graduate of Golden Gate Baptist Seminary, who had also been encouraged by the work and influence of Francis DuBose, became interested in reaching out to the hippie converts to Christ. Dr. DuBose and his wonderful wife Dorothy, who were members of Pastor Gossett's church, provided much support and encouragement.

Soul Inn was born out of Lincoln Park Baptist Church (SBC) within a relatively short time. It may be that it was the first such Christian commune on the West Coast. Among the many people who were becoming Christians were a significant number who were homeless, so beginning the communes came naturally, even out of necessity.

Soul Inn's opening night was quite unforgettable. The Salvation Army had donated bunk beds and blankets to us, which we set up in the very limited Sunday school space at the store front church. On the corner of what I think was Haight Street and Clayton, at about 4:00 PM each day, a grass roots organization of Hippies called the Diggers set up a card table and tried to steer people into finding food, shelter, and medical help. For weeks I had been stopping by and telling the Diggers that we would soon open Soul Inn. Finally the day arrived, and I made the grand announcement.

That evening, four of us were sitting around a makeshift table, a sheet of plywood sitting on the backs of four chairs. Dave Palma, Paul Finn, Roy, and I were talking about spending our first night at the Soul Inn. It was late—a winter night—and our only remaining food was a small amount of pork and beans left in a quart can. That was it, no other food except some Lipton tea bags. It must have been about 10:00 PM, and there was a knock on the door. Outside stood twenty-six youngish hippies who had just walked several miles to Balboa Street between 42nd and 43rd Avenues in the Richmond District. The Diggers had given out the address as we requested, but now what were we to do with all these people? Paul Finn and I went back into the kitchen or what passed for one, and started scooping pork and beans into paper bowls. Within a very short time both of us realized we were in the middle of a miracle. There was enough in the can to feed *all twenty-six people*, with as much left as when we started. I scooped, and

Paul carried the bowls in. Twenty-six bowls filled with pork and beans that came out of what had been a nearly empty quart can. That was only one of what would be many miracles, no two identical, but happening when we least expected and most needed them. There were miracles of healing that were plain and incontrovertible—not a large number, and they did not happen as seen on television. For whatever reason, I tended to play down the miracles, knowing from the biblical gospel writers that Jesus had done the same. As time went on, I realized why Jesus did not publicize or sensationalize miracles—strange and dangerous results often follow. But there were indeed miracles.

More Christian houses

As time went on, more and more young people were becoming Christians, and the need for housing grew. The Soul Inn was the first answer to this need, but many followed. For a while, I kept track in a journal of the different people who lived with my family in our Zion's Inn in San Rafael, and the number of those who flowed into and out of that house was significant. Sometime in 1969 we formed a non-profit corporation called House Ministries, through the volunteer labor of lawyer Chuck Kopp, in order to bring form and structure to the growing number of what we called Christian Houses. One of the first books I wrote was an operation manual for the leaders of our Christian houses. These houses stretched from Sonoma County to San Jose, and finally to the Walnut Creek area of the East Bay. David Hoyt started Christian Houses in some of these areas, then moved to Atlanta, Georgia and opened up Christian Houses in nine southern states. From time to time, I would visit David in Atlanta and traveled to some of the surrounding houses. Christian Houses began springing up all over the country by 1969.

Lonnie Frisbee and Chuck Smith

One such house was The House of Miracles in Costa Mesa. One of the young men who had been a part of The Living Room outreach with Ted Wise was Lonnie Frisbee. Lonnie was younger than the rest of the group, nearer my age, and he loved to talk theology and the Bible and to roam the streets of the Haight to witness to the hippies about Jesus. On many occasions I watched Lonnie begin a simple conversation with one hippie which then turned into a preaching event, with cars stopping and blocking streets. After a while, Lonnie desired to get back home to Costa Mesa. Shortly after his move he called and asked me and several others to come down to the House of Miracles to interview some Christians with whom he was thinking of joining forces.

David Hoyt, Danny Sands, Rick Sacks, and I drove down to Costa Mesa and met with Chuck Smith and a number of his elders or deacons. Pastor Smith wore a shirt and tie, as did the rest who were with him. They sat on the furniture, while we Jesus Freaks sat on the floor. For some period there were questions and answers, and theology was discussed. In the end the four of us advised Lonnie that he should develop a relationship with these more experienced men and cooperate with them. This subsequently turned out to have been a significant event in the history of the JPM.

Shortly after Chuck Smith and his leaders left, Lonnie wanted to drive to Newport Beach to look at a Christian group that had begun a kind of Christian nightclub. It was that very night that we encountered David Berg—the soon-to-be leader of a cult that would be known as The Children of God—a Bible-based cult that David Hoyt ended up joining.

David "Mo" Berg

David Berg, with at least two of his own kids, met with us outside the back of the nightclub. It was an unusual ministry, risky and edgy by the standards of the day, and the place was packed with young people. Berg and company were dressed in black suits and ties. They appeared clean cut, proper and respectable, and they made it plain they did not like us; we made it plain we did not like them either. We parted company after a few minutes, but we would never forget the encounter.

A second notable miracle

(It is not my intent to focus on miracles, but they did occur, and I have selected only a few as illustrations.) After David Hoyt and his wife Victoria moved to Walnut Creek to found another Christian house, Living Streams, the Philpotts—wife Bobbie, young daughters Dory and Grace, and our new born, Vernon—were now alone with two or three young women in our Zion's Inn for girls at 128 Greenfield Avenue in San Rafael, Marin County. For income, I had been painting houses with David, and when he left for Walnut Creek the work dwindled. The situation grew worse and soon became dire. I must relate the next story, though due to its rather fantastic nature, I rarely speak of it for fear that people will think I am somewhat deranged. There was, however, a miracle breakfast.

One morning all of our family and the residents of our house were gathered around the kitchen table with nothing to eat—I mean nothing at all. There were a few tea bags, so Bobbie made tea. Sitting around the table we looked at each other, trying to make the best of it, and I can still remember the awful sense of failure that came over me. Before me were my two little girls with nothing to eat and nothing to pack in their school lunch boxes. Then there was a knock on the door. Two people, a married couple I thought, stood there with bags in their hands. I had never seen them before and I would never see them again. No names were exchanged, rather they handed us the bags and promptly left. Inside were containers of hot food—bacon, eggs, potatoes, orange juice, coffee, and milk. Just enough for all of us. That is just how it happened. Oddly, we were not able to identify any restaurant or grocery store from which the food could have come; there were no markings on the packages. It happened only once, but it was a tremendous relief to me and the rest of the household.

A para-church ministry

Our work centered on Bible studies and evangelistic outreaches at the local high schools and the one college in Marin County, College of Marin in Kentfield. Eventually we had a Bible study in each school. We opened up one Christian house after the other; I signed so many leases and guaranteed so many utility accounts that it caused me some sleepless nights. We opened up Christian bookstores and even a thrift shop.

On Sunday mornings my family and I would attend local Baptist churches, mostly SBC aligned churches and some ABC churches as well. In every case we were warmly received and encouraged. Though we were ministering alongside churches and were not a church, I felt it important to be a part of a community of faith; evangelistic outreach was not enough. Mostly we attended the First Baptist Church of San Rafael on Lincoln Avenue, the Lucas Valley Community Church in a northern suburb of San Rafael, and the First Baptist Church of Novato.

This was during a period in my life when I was attempting to copy the example of George Mueller of Bristol who never disclosed his needs or those of the orphanage he had started in Bristol, England, but only told his heavenly Father what he needed. Until the painting work took hold (story below) such praying, and the answers thereto, was the only resource I had. It was 1969 and the ministry was exploding; we were in the midst of what would later be called the JPM, and I had no time to make any money, though that would soon change, as I will relate next.

Work Crews

It became apparent that the work that was growing up around us needed to be financed in some way. Despite answers to prayer, as related above, I was not always able to follow the example of George Mueller. During my travels, I kept the names and addresses of many people, and from that list I began sending out a monthly newsletter that continued until 1980. This newsletter eventually brought in about $600 a month.

In the Christian houses were young people who were capable of working, so we went at it. Through David I had learned how to paint houses, and we began to organize paint crews. We had several students attending Golden Gate Baptist Seminary in Mill Valley associated with our ministry who also learned how to paint, and we ran ads in the local Marin Independent Journal that read "Seminary Student and Crew." At the height of it we had three painting crews and one construction crew lead by Mark Buckley. Much of the time the houses had more than adequate amounts of money and the members of the houses decided where to give excess funds.

The work crews were discipleship programs in action, teaching many marginal people how to work and manage their money. It also served as a foundation for many young families.

Joyful Noise

Music, predominantly guitar music, was prominent in the JPM. Early in 1968 I began to learn to play the guitar, never picking up bass or lead, but I learned just enough chords to play most of the Jesus songs. During that period, I wrote a few simple choruses and am gratified that some of them are still sung to this day.

At Excelsior Baptist Church in Byron we sang hymns with a piano accompanying. The same had been true at First Baptist at Fairfield. At the Bible studies, however, the guitar was the instrument of choice, and the music was modeled on the rock and roll we had all grown up with. Quickly, bands emerged that mostly wrote and played their own songs, and we formed one out of my Tuesday night Bible study called Joyful Noise. Greg Beamer, Rick Ricketts, Kenny Sanders, Jeanine Wright, Donna Hays, Malcolm Dawes, Tommy Gaulden, Gary Bartholomew, Jimmy Ayala, Linda Fritz Patton, Mary Kay Herb, Mark Buckley, Chris Kenner, Kenny Hopkins, and others made up Joyful Noise over a period of four years. I played rhythm guitar and sang lead. (Oddly, my childhood severe ear infections served me well in Joyful Noise and as a preacher, because to compensate for my hearing loss I developed a loud, strong voice.)

The years of the ministry of Joyful Noise were undoubtedly the most productive and fun years of my life. We were not good at all, but we wrote most of our own music and were equipped to play anywhere, anytime. We played at nearly all the high schools in Marin County, at many churches, and on the street, in parks, private homes, and even once in San Quentin State Prison.

Joyful Noise had a growing reputation for performing and preaching at drug abuse assemblies in high schools. The band would set up and quickly play a song or two, songs like *You'll Never Get to Heaven on LSD; Oh Holy Joe; The Christian Way of Life; There's a Great Day Coming; One Name; Jesus, Jesus, When I Hear that Golden Name;* and *This Little Light of Mine.* Then one of us would give a testimony, followed by another song or two, then another testimony, until I would finally preach a short sermon and give the standard appeal. Time and again, nearly the entire audience to whom we were singing would apparently be converted. One event stands out in my mind.

A Glenn County high school in Northern California invited us to spend an entire day at their high school of 95 students. Besides the assembly where we played our music and gave our testimonies, we split up into groups of two and visited every classroom for more testimonies and Q and A. At the end of the day we totaled up lists of names of 96 people who had made a commitment to Christ, one more than the student body. I sent these names and addresses with phone numbers to a local ministerial association for follow up. It was quite a ride home for Joyful Noise.

Due to the influence of Cora Vance, a wonderful Christian lady I had met at a Women's charismatic meeting where I had spoken in Atlanta, Georgia, the Atlanta school district hired us to conduct drug abuse assemblies at each of their high schools. It took us three weeks to complete the circuit, holding at least two assemblies each day. On one such occasion, our assembly was scheduled during first period in the school's gym. We lost our way and arrived late. When we opened the door to the gym we found it packed, wall to wall, with kids sitting silently, patiently, on the benches—at least 2,000 of them. In the silence we set up. Guitars were not in tune, we had no time to warm up instruments or voices, and the time was slipping away. We were introduced, I made some sort of apology for being late, opened up with a couple of songs but done so badly I knew we had to shut down.

One of our Joyful Noise crew, a seventeen year old newcomer named Kenny Hopkins, stepped forward to sing and play *Jesus, Jesus, When I Hear that Golden Name.* It is a slow, quiet, meditative song, almost like a love song to Jesus, and when Kenny was finished he said a few words and stepped back. The time was gone, the bell for the second period was ringing, and I simply asked anyone who wanted to be a follower of Jesus to stand up. The entire place responded, teachers and students alike. No sound, no excitement—my few sentences lasted less than a minute. Even today it thrills me. At this point in my life I would not count all those who stood to have been converted. Also, I recognize that I might have even contributed to a false sense of eternal security for some. Yet, in the JPM the Spirit of God was poured out in unusual ways. I do not say this to justify my actions, and later on such thinking was used to rationalize quite bizarre behavior and theology, but times of awakening are not like normal times.

For four years requests for Joyful Noise came in. More requests were turned down than accepted—and only because of lack of time. We never charged for this ministry, but food, gas, and lodging money had a way of showing up. Once we spent a week at the University of Texas in Austin for a student-led religious week, sponsored by the Southern Baptist Student Union there. Maranatha, the lead band from Calvary Chapel, led by Chuck Girard, was also there that week. They were very good musically, and we were not, but it did not matter, as we saw many conversions during that week.

Requests for Joyful Noise slowed and finally stopped altogether, and so we disbanded. That was 1972.

Psychedelic conversions?

As stated earlier, a song Joyful Noise played was titled, "You'll Never Get to Heaven on LSD," and the lyrics then ran, "You can go pretty far and fly pretty high, but you'll never get to heaven on LSD."

Early hippies preached that through drugs like LSD, mescaline, peyote, marijuana, and others, the mind could be expanded, the consciousness attuned to fantastic spiritual experiences, and a new generation would usher in a new world built upon love and peace. However, that notion lost steam fairly early on as minds were shattered and broken instead of achieving a high level of awareness. For a couple of years I made it a point to visit the locked psych wards at San Francisco General Hospital and talked to some of the kids whose minds were blown. I saw the results of psychedelic drugs first hand. (I was surprised that the staff would allow me to roam through the wards and evangelize their patients, but they did, and often I would spend hours doing personal evangelism in full view of everyone.)

One of the places I routinely visited in the Haight-Ashbury was the Switchboard. It was a hippie-run organization that tried to provide for the physical needs of all the hippie kids coming to San Francisco from all over the country. One of their specialties was to provide "trip masters" for kids during their first LSD experiences and help them through a wild ride. Often I would talk to these trip masters, who thought very highly of themselves and, who I happened to know, took sexual advantage of some of the stoned kids. I gave them so much trouble about their criminal activity that I was finally barred from coming on the property.

Once in a while someone would tell me that they encountered Jesus or an angel or Satan on a trip. My answer was that it was the devil maybe, but not Jesus. The Jesus People Movement was not built around psychedelic conversions; not even close. Not all of the Jesus People were out of the hippie scene. Many who came to Christ in those years were ordinary middle class kids who never did get involved in the hippie lifestyle.

On the road

In the fall of 1968 Paul Bryant, Oliver Heath, and I set out for Mobile, Alabama in Ollie's new red Volkswagen bug. The little car was stuffed with printed material to be handed out along the way. On the road we stopped at every college or university we came across. I would haul out my guitar, set up someplace on campus, sing some songs, and preach a while when a crowd gathered. Our California license plates were usually enough to attract attention, but I looked somewhat like a hippie, and in many of the places we visited few had ever seen a hippie up close. After the short preaching, we would hand out literature and talk individually with those who would do so. At Hardin-Simmons University in Abilene, Texas, a Southern Baptist school, we were ordered off the campus and threatened with arrest. But after some pressure from the students, the school officials understood we really were Christians and not trouble makers and made an abrupt turn and welcomed us.

Secular schools all along our route received us to some degree. Of course, with them it was always the One Way theology that got us in trouble. Joyful Noise also traveled far and wide, and the trips we made were often quite eventful. During this period I was invited to various places to speak to one group or another and had opportunities to visit Jesus People in areas far from San Francisco.

After David Hoyt moved to Atlanta, Georgia sometime in early 1969, I began visiting him, and then came into contact with Jesus People throughout the southern states. Then I made friends with a runaway from Mercer Island, a suburb of Seattle, Washington, and soon became acquainted with Jesus People in the Pacific Northwest. Los Angeles was never forgotten, and I often returned there to spend time with Jesus People in that area, preaching from time to time at His Place on the Strip, operated either by Arthur Blessit or Dywane Peterson.

What I found was that what we had developed in San Francisco and surrounding counties—the Bible studies, Christian houses, street evangelism featuring personal witnessing and literature distribution, and music bands—were springing up in locations everywhere. In general, the first awakening's dominant expression was solid gospel preaching done by ordained preachers. The first half of the second awakening was the same. In the third awakening the focus was the prayer meeting with exhortations, prayers, and testimonies. The JPM was a little different; it was youth-oriented, both in terms of those presenting the gospel and those receiving it, and its principle venue was the streets of America's cities.

After 1970 a degree of organization crept into the JPM. There were conferences and large campouts featuring music and preaching. In the Bay Area there were several times when JPM leaders met together to plan evangelistic outreaches, much of which was stimulated by or held in conjunction with the Christian World Liberation Front lead by Jack Sparks, Pat

Matriciana, Brooks Alexander, and Billy Squires, among others. But when Moishe Rosen showed up in the days before he founded Jews for Jesus, he and I together organized large scale events involving hundreds of Jesus People. Once Moishe (I knew him as Martin then) and I agreed to descend on San Francisco's Broadway Street in North Beach to create a stir and promote an event where Hal Lindsay of *The Late Great Planet Earth* fame was to preach in front of Big Al's. In two days we mustered a couple hundred Jesus People from our Marin County base alone and set them to working up dozens of placards and hundreds of "broad sides" (tracts). This, however, was as close as the Jesus People that I was involved with arrived at any kind of organization.

Toward the close of the awakening

Those of us who were involved in the JPM did not have any idea that anything as grand and historic as an awakening was going on; I certainly did not. I knew about the American awakenings from the class in Church History taught at Golden Gate Seminary by Dr. Jack Manning, but it was not apparent to me or anyone else whom I knew that *this* was an awakening. What we experienced at the time were hundreds, even thousands, of mostly young people coming to Jesus for salvation, accompanied by the occurrence of various signs and wonders. Almost everything we did seemed to turn out wonderfully well. Teen-age kids with little or no Bible training experienced great success in evangelism. Runaways and "dopers" found themselves leading hundreds of eager followers of Jesus. Dozens, eventually hundreds, of offbeat ministries ranging from Christian houses, ranches, coffeehouses, restaurants, bookstores, missionary teams, and other evangelistic outreaches emerged seemingly overnight.

Those of us who had not come from pentecostal backgrounds and who were only tangentially associated with the charismatic movement, still engaged in or witnessed healings and demons being cast out of people. For me, it was only at the Anchor Rescue Mission that I participated in what is normally associated with pentecostals. I was a Baptist, still am, and I did not appreciate pentecostals much, because they were always trying to get me to speak in tongues (prior to when this gift was actually given to me).[49] I never did adopt the traditional pentecostal theology, and the signs and wonders I saw were always in direct connection with the preaching of the gospel.

Then, sometime after 1972, I began to notice that the miracles we had become accustomed to were absent much of the time, even in the context of strong gospel preaching; and the number of converts was dwindling. Whereas a simple gospel presentation had previously resulted in large audiences and dozens of conversions, the crowds were getting smaller, and the response was becoming meager. We closed Christian houses, bookstores, and churches. We did not know it, but the JPM was over, at least for us.

If we had known the nature of a true, God-sent revival, much of the excesses that followed the JPM might not have occurred. We assumed that what we were experiencing was normal. We reasoned that this is how it was and always would be—many conversions with signs and wonders. No techniques, no money, often no buildings, no publicity, no training—just the mighty wind of the Holy Spirit. When it all stopped, we were at a loss. Had we known we had been living through an awakening, we might have adjusted. However, we did not adjust; instead we wanted more of the same. We

---

49 In 1968, some months prior to the establishment of Soul Inn, while sleeping behind the pulpit at Lincoln Park Baptist Church, at 2:00 AM, I awoke speaking loudly in tongues—at least as far as I know it was speaking in tongues. My guess is that it was my "baptism in the Holy Spirit." Though I had been baptized into the Body of Christ at my conversion, yet this was apart and distinct from that. Things changed for me after this experience. It was as Jesus had stated in Acts 1:8: the Holy Spirit empowered me to do the work I was called to. Not that people were not being converted, they were, but now there was something more. Now the healings, the casting out of demons, and more, would become commonplace and did continue until sometime in the mid-1970s. It has been decades since I have spoken in tongues, but I do not discount the reality of the charismatic gifts.

wanted the excitement, the crowds, the attention, and the success. So, never mind the Holy Spirit, some of us set about to have it anyway we could get it.

The Dark Side of the Jesus People Movement

Prophecy, signs, wonders, and healing

Somewhere around 1971 an intense interest in predictive prophecy swept over the Jesus People in the Bay Area—and elsewhere, of course. We would gather people around us, lay our hands on them, and *prophesy* over them. Many would wait in long lines for this experience. It was indeed an intoxicating ministry. Here we were telling people what to do with their lives: "You should drop out of college and go into the ministry." "You have been called by God to be a missionary." "You are to marry Johnny and raise up a dozen children dedicated to the Lord." And all this would be punctuated with, "Thus sayeth the Lord." Heady stuff, and those who earned the designation of *prophet* amongst us were held in high esteem, including me.

From somewhere and someone I learned how to impress people with my prophecies. I started saying things like, "God gave me a word for you." Or it might be, "God woke me up this morning and gave me a word for you." Few questioned this.

At a funeral some years ago, a woman approached me and began to berate me. She told me that I had prophesied that she should marry a certain young man, which she did, and with whom she eventually had two children. Her husband, from whom she was now divorced, was in prison, convicted of sexually molesting their children. I could give other examples but I will not.

I probably prophesied to hundreds of people during the course of my misunderstanding of the gift of prophecy. And I am not alone; in fact, I was a minor player in this. It still goes on—people love to be told what to do, and Christian-based people will turn to the prophet rather than the psychic; now

I wonder if there was, or is, much difference. This error tarnished the JPM and was responsible for the darkest excesses of it.

We also engaged in what we called "deliverance" ministry—that is, we cast demons out of people. Our theology was that a Christian could have an indwelling unclean spirit, having been invaded by a demon prior to conversion. We looked for certain activities in the life of a person—occult practices, the use of psychedelics, and other sometimes innocent forays into the demonic realms. This was a major facet of our ministry, and I took a major lead in it. Though it was controversial, and I am unsure today of some aspects of the theology of it, I maintain that it was a valid ministry. Without exaggeration, I would estimate that thousands of demons were cast out of hundreds of people over the course of those years, and the result was usually life-enhancing for the persons involved. This is one part of the ministry occurring during the JPM from which I will not retreat. In fact, I will engage in this ministry today.[50]

Early in the JPM I observed what I still believe were genuine healings, which included healing of structural damage, such as broken bones and diseased organs, and not exclusively healing of that which might be psycho-somatic in nature. I am tempted to give an illustration or two, and I have some vivid memories to rely on, but I will simply say that we saw that Jesus healed people and cast out demons in the Scripture, and we thought it perfectly proper that this ministry would be continued into our own period of history. Additionally, we read that such ministry took place in the Book of Acts as well as in Jesus' ministry, so we expected it and believed God would do it. There were two occasions where I was healed

---

50 I am uncertain whether a Christian can become indwelt by a demon, and there is a question of whether or not a Christian can have an indwelling demon or not. The simple fact was that all, or nearly all, of those who requested deliverance ministry were Christians, or so they and we believed. For a more complete discussion of the subject of casting out of demons see How Christians Cast Out Demons Today, published by Earthen Vessel Publishing, 2009 and available at www.earthenvessel.net.

myself, both of which were very concrete and without emotion, and both were private—I was the only one present.

The healings and the casting out of demons accompanied gospel preaching. I began to see this in 1968, and I was not prepared for it. As a Southern Baptist seminary student, these things had not been a part of my experience. As I have pointed out, because signs and wonders followed the ministry of Jesus, Paul, and Peter, the Jesus People thought it was normative. Now I see that it was part of the outpouring of the Holy Spirit in that fourth awakening, because once the awakening came to a conclusion, the signs and wonders slowed in frequency and eventually ceased altogether. Today, in these *normal* times, there are still healings and demons are cast out, but nothing like what I saw from 1968 to 1972. I propose that this is characteristic of other awakenings as well and lends credence to the idea that the JPM fits the criteria for it being an awakening alongside the other three.

The Children of God

A most dangerous cult to emerge during the JPM was headed by David "Moses" or "Mo" Berg, whom David Hoyt and I had encountered in Newport Beach, California, at the behest of Lonnie Frisbee. At some point, Berg had become indwelt by a spirit that named itself Abraham or something close to that spelling. This spirit's modus operandi was to dictate "Mo Letters," whose content and its application quickly transformed a group of hippie Christians into what became called "'The Children of God" (from here on COG), something far from normal Christianity.

For a detailed description of COG see Don Lattin's *Jesus Freaks: A True story of Murder and Madness on the Evangelical Edge*, published by HarperCollins Publishers, 2007. Mr. Lattin spoke with me during the writing of his book, and I loaned him several dozen of Berg's Mo Letters. One letter was titled, *Flirty Little Fishes*, in which the spirit within Berg cleverly suggested that female COG members should sexually entice young men into the organization. I saw this very technique employed by COG members on one of my trips to England.

David Hoyt left for Atlanta, Georgia, after his ministry in Walnut Creek could be turned over to others. David and I had often talked about Berg and his followers; we stood firmly against them and did what we could to warn other Jesus People around the country about them. The COG were preying on Jesus People and filling their ranks with them. Their message was simple and alluring: leave everything behind and follow Jesus, deny yourself and take up the cross. Many succumbed to the message, which sounded biblical enough on the surface. What really lurked under that surface, however, was a group under strict cultic control, led to greater and greater extremes by a man who was listening to and obeying a demonic spirit-guide. David and I were both alert to the danger.

One evening in 1970 I received a call from Ed Sweeney, a Catholic priest who ministered in Atlanta. I had met him at a Catholic charismatic gathering a year or two earlier. Father Sweeney informed me that David Hoyt, his wife, his children, and his entire ministry in Atlanta—about two hundred young people—had boarded buses owned by the COG and had allowed themselves to be taken to a large COG enclave somewhere in Texas.

After a red-eye flight to Atlanta, I arrived at day break, was greeted at the airport by Ed, who drove us to the former French Embassy that had been David's headquarters. After they prevented me from entering the house, a young man came out onto the porch to talk with me. He had been in the COG for six months, and as we talked, I felt the nearly overwhelming desire to join the COG! If it had not been for Ed literally dragging me away and into his car, I might have disappeared into that cult, as did David and his family.

It was several years before I saw David again, though after a year with COG, he began writing to me. I knew it would only be a matter of time before David would run afoul of the COG leaders and be expelled. Sure enough, around 1973 I received an invitation from David to join him and a ministry under the sponsorship of Kenneth Frampton. I was asked to come to London for a period of time and pastor a group of Jesus People from Milwaukee who had been stranded but befriended by Mr. Frampton. This was the first of several lengthy trips to England that I undertook over the next six years.

David has come out of the COG, but sadly, some members of his family did not. It would take decades before the entire family was out from under the control of the Berg cult. Much healing remains to be done, but David and I now enjoy a stronger fellowship than ever before. And David, despite it all, continues to be a faithful follower of Jesus along with his wonderful wife Ginny.

The COG brought much grief to the JPM, because most people were not able to differentiate them from the mainstream of the JPM. The media seemed to love the COG, and over the years I had to defend my ministry and myself to those who thought the antics of the COG was the norm for the JPM.

Jim Jones and the People's Temple

Another spiritual leader and his group also had many people fooled as to their real nature. Jim Jones did not impact my ministry in Marin County until 1972, when Church of the Open Door was established—a non-denominational, charismatic church built on the ministry foundation that several of us had established in Marin's towns. I had become aware of Jones from reading articles in the *San Francisco Chronicle*, since he had become involved in San Francisco's politics, which were quite strange during that period.

Jones had begun sending buses to our church parking lot in San Rafael on Sunday mornings to pick up any of our attendees who wanted to come to his services instead. This tactic revealed Jones' arrogant and aggressive nature. At first I did nothing to stop the sheep-stealing, but after hearing reports of what was taking place at the meetings, I decided to visit The People's Temple myself; in fact, I attended several services.

What I recount now may seem rather strange, and what I experienced was shared by others and over an extended period of time. Here is what happened: one, angel wings (or so it was said) brushed over me; two, my up-reached hand was clasped as in a hand shake by another hand that I could feel but not see; three, throughout the room wafted a pleasant aroma, which Jim Jones called "the sweet savor of the Lord;" four, drops of oil fell on the Bible held open on my lap. Then there was a young black girl from Oakland, maybe aged thirteen, who often stood in front of the congregation as the "stigmata" appeared on her hands and ankles—those places where the Roman soldiers pounded the nails into Jesus' body.

After this I understood the attraction; there was a strong spiritual presence in Jim Jones' meetings. However, there was no indication that the gospel was preached or the Bible taught. Christian language was spoken, hymns were sung, prayers were prayed, but it was beyond anything pentecostal or charismatic that I had ever seen.

When the Jonestown tragedy in Guiana became known to the world, and for some months after that, I officiated at funerals for some of those who died at Jonestown. It was then that I was able to make sense of what had happened: there was at work at The People's Temple that which had also been at work with David Moses Berg and COG—a demonic power that was able to seduce and deceive through counterfeit signs and wonders. I had felt that power that morning in Atlanta, and I had seen it at work at The People's Temple—it was that same drawing I had experienced during the kirtans at the Hare Krishna temple in 1967.

This was a dark side indeed. Not all that is spiritual is of the Spirit of God, and with our charismatic orientation, many of us were not able to grasp this. This failure was likely the major aspect of the dark side of the JPM; we did not know that prophecy, healings, and miracles could be of a devilish origin. We had experienced some of these directly and thought them to be genuine. Currently, in my spiritual walk I am still working through aspects of this; I do not want to assign all signs and wonders to the nether regions, because I think that during times of awakening there are exceptional Holy Spirit gifts given that do authentically result in glory to God. Let me be clear, however, that what I experienced during the Hindu services, or observed at The People's Temple, or felt that awful morning in Atlanta with the COG—none were from the Spirit of God.

The Shepherding Movement

Perhaps more devastating to the JPM than the COG, Jim Jones, or any number of other strange teachings and groups like the Manifested Sons of God, was what came to be called the Shepherding Movement. The Fort Lauderdale Five—Bob Mumford, Charles Simpson, Derek Prince, Don Basham, and Ern Baxter, all respected teachers in the early years of the JPM—began to form an umbrella type of ministry that seemed to them to be a necessity, given the chaotic and confused nature of the JPM. These five leaders began to accumulate churches and ministries under their authority and over which they became overseers or "shepherds" of what became rather large church conglomerates. It seemed almost a natural kind of progression, a helpful ministry, one borne out of caring, and I think that at first it was.

Many considered it to be desirable to be accountable to Bob Mumford or one of the other shepherds. Across the country, Jesus People leaders with their ministries and churches *submitted* themselves to one of the five shepherds and then themselves became "under-shepherds." I considered doing the same myself for all of the Open Door churches, because the work was often times beyond me and left me wondering what to do next. Here was where my characteristic independent streak rescued me from submitting to men. There was something I rebelled against in the Shepherding Movement, and this was misunderstood by many of those who served in leadership with me.

My decision was that local leadership was more biblical, despite the troubles we faced. Finally, one of our pastors, a former seminary student who had taken over the remains of several Christian houses, a bookstore, and our church in San Francisco, announced he was submitted to Bob Mumford. The battle lines were now drawn. At that point I wrote a pamphlet about the movement and pointed out that the leaders would "wine and dine" pastors and others, in order to get them to submit. This little booklet was printed by many groups over the years and was particularly used in Great Britain where the Shepherding Movement was starting to make inroads.

The Shepherding Movement was the source of a great deal of grief for me and does continue to impact me in subtle ways to this very day. It fractured alliances and friendships and, from my perspective, may have been one reason the JPM ended, in our part of the country at minimum, but to some extent throughout the entire nation.

The Shepherding Movement eventually imploded somewhere in the late 1970s or early 1980s. I recall running into Bob Mumford while he and I were both doing volunteer work with the Protestant Chapel at San Quentin Prison. Bob invited me to his office, and we had a wonderful time of reconciliation. Bob was very open about the error of the Shepherding Movement and did ask for forgiveness, which I was heartened to extend.

One more thought on the dark side

When the JPM ended, few knew what was taking place. The signs and wonders were gone and so were most of the conversions. It was as though life had returned to normal, and many of us did not know how to live in that world. The Bible studies were not the same; few even requested healing. Those who sought deliverance from evil spirits became fewer and fewer. No one wanted a San Francisco Jesus Freak to speak to their youth group anymore. The times, they were a-changing.

Whether history will verify this following evaluation or not, I do not know of course, nevertheless I have wondered if the efforts at creating revival and conversions that followed the JPM was little more than well-intentioned human engineering. I am referring specifically to some aspects of the church growth movement, the seeker sensitive movement, or perhaps even what is called the "emerging church" movement.

In 1986 and 1987 my denomination sent me to Fuller Seminary in Pasadena, California, to attend the beginning conference for church growth, then a year later to attend the advanced conference. I learned tactics on how to get people into the pews and applied them as best I could at Miller Avenue Baptist Church—with some success. But I knew the difference and knew it was not the same as what happens in a God-breathed revival. Eventually, I discarded the techniques and went back to gospel preaching and Bible teaching, though still lacking the results experienced during the JPM.

The bright side of the Jesus People Movement

The full story of the impact of the JPM, or what I call here the "bright side" of the JPM, is yet to be fully understood and evaluated. This present account is heavily subjective, since it is drawn from my doubtlessly very limited perspective. However, many people were definitely converted to Christ. How many is completely unknown. In Marin County, my guess is a number of approximately five hundred. In the early years in San Francisco, my guess is a number of several hundred runaways and hippie types were born from above. In the areas I visited around California, and in states between California and Georgia where I traveled on road trips, the number is perhaps several thousand, maybe more. As for conversions due to literature and Bible distribution, there is no way to know. Many churches were formed, some small denominations were developed, and hundreds of Christian houses were begun, though most have closed by now. I can testify to many dozens of former Jesus People who have contacted me over the years, and a common question is, "Are you still following Jesus?"

Just recently, I received a wonderful CD from Paul Finn in New York; on it he reads, so very well, the names of God. He was the one who was dishing up the pork and beans with me at Soul Inn in San Francisco when we witnessed the multiplication of food. (Paul called me some years back, and I asked him what he remembered about that night; his report jived perfectly with my own recollections.) Paul and his friend Dave Palma, who was also there that miracle night, went back home to New York, and each founded a Christian house. One was called The House of Philadelphia and the other Philadelphia House—both in the confines of New York City. Yes, the Jesus People!

People I have known from the JPM have gone on to become pastors and missionaries. Instead of dropping out, they went to college, became productive in the work force, and started families. There are also sad stories of those who have stumbled and of those who have fallen away and no longer consider themselves Christians. I am aware of very few of these, but their stories and the bigger story are not yet fully written.

As I come in contact with people who had been part of the JPM in various parts of America, I find the same thing— converted people still following Jesus. In my travels during the JPM, I visited large cities as well as small towns, and I would find Jesus People there. It was all across the country, seemingly sprouting up all at once or at least very close in time. What has been or will yet be the impact of all those who were swept up into the Kingdom of God? Their stories have yet to be told and may never be.

It is impossible to know what America would look like without the JPM. My sense of it is that the dire consequences that followed the Vietnam War, the sexual revolution, and the beginnings of a mammoth drug culture have been greatly cushioned by the JPM. It could have been worse.

The Jesus People Movement— A Fourth Great Awakening?

It is generally recognized that America has experienced three great awakenings. The first occurred from roughly 1734 to 1742. Some of the major preachers were Jonathan Edwards, George Whitefield, John Wesley, Samuel Davies, Jonathan Dickinson, Gilbert Tennent, and many others. The second occurred from roughly 1799 to 1835. Timothy Dwight and Ashael Nettleton were prominent during the first half of this awakening, as were Barton Stone and Peter Cartwright. Charles Finney is associated with the second half of that awakening. The third awakening is usually placed in the years 1857 to 1858 or longer (perhaps running throughout the entire length of the Civil War). Jeremiah Lamphier, Henry Ward Beecher, and Phoebe Palmer were noted leaders during the third great awakening. The first and third great awakenings spread to other countries, notably Great Britain.

It is generally held, though there were major leaders associated with the awakenings, that no one is regarded as the progenitor of the awakenings. The awakenings were underway before names and places were attached to them. The awakenings were not the result of human engineering or scheming. They began and they ended. No methods of stimulation were used for exciting the awakenings except prayer, stories of conversion, and some advertising announcements. Preaching and prayer were essentially the only means used at gatherings. Sermons centered on the grace of God in Christ, the sovereign power of God, the inability of a person to come to Christ on his/her own, the cross and Jesus' shed blood for the forgiveness of sin, the resurrection, and the sure reality of judgment and hell.

The JPM preachers and witnesses focused on themes similar to those of the great awakenings. A rough approximation of the standard evangelical, pre-millennial model was generally accepted, and the Arminian position (as compared to Calvinist) was dominant. The major evangelical, biblical themes were characteristic of the movement, though there were variations in what may be called fringe areas. *Jesus and the cross* were the chief preaching points. People would be converted in many ways, not just at the altar call. I recall times when people would appear to become converted during the singing of choruses or while attending a somber Bible study. Evangelism came in many forms.

Murray's marks

Iain H. Murray, in *Revival and Revivalism*, lists marks of the 1858 awakening that I think are common to any true spiritual awakening. Murray's list is substantially as follows:

> hunger for the Word of God; (2) hunger for prayer; (3) hunger for serious Christian literature; (4) a sense of wonder and profound seriousness; (5) the same work evident in many places at once; (6) joyful praise and readiness to witness; (7) a new energy in practical Christian service; (8) the recovery of family worship and family religion; and (9) an observable raising of the whole moral tone of society.[51]

Iain H. Murray stated that hunger for the Word of God is characteristic of revival (#1 in list above). This was certainly true of the JPM. The Bible study became the hallmark of the JPM. This is where fellowship was centered, this is where the

---
51   Murray, *Revivals and Revivalism*, 348.

gospel was preached, and this is where people testified as to their conversion. Baptisms were conducted during or after Bible studies; sometimes the Lord's Supper was taken. There was always the need for more Bible study leaders and places to hold the studies. The Bible studies spread rapidly and were very popular, even amongst non-believers and seekers. Bible studies were held in schools, even during school hours, on fields, in parks, on the beach, on the street, in homes, and in rented halls and churches. The format was mostly verse-by-verse exposition, and the sessions were long—two hours in length was not unusual. There also were prayers and simple choruses sung to guitar accompaniment.

However they were called—"Jesus kids," "Jesus freaks," or "Jesus people" —they would carry their Bibles with them wherever they went. Some would have to be exhorted to tend to the necessities of life and limit their Bible study time. The favorite translation was the King James Version, and some even peppered their conversation with "thees" and "thous." Bible memorization was common, and some Jesus people learned whole books of the Bible by heart. Some of them loved nothing better than to spend the day and the night looking into the Scripture.

Then secondly, Murray said that hunger for prayer is characteristic of revival. This was also true of the JPM. There were all night prayer meetings. Bible studies and prayer went naturally together and were foundations of the JPM. It was usually intense prayer with no care about what others thought of the style of praying or content of the prayer. Jesus People often prayed to the exclusion of other, practical responsibilities.

Murray said that there is also a hunger for serious Christian literature. We read John Wesley's journals, Martin Luther, Augustine, R.A. Torrey, Billy Graham, Charles Finney, C.H. Spurgeon, John Calvin, Andrew Murray, Watchman Nee, C.S. Lewis, and many others. Thomas a Kempis' *Imitation of Christ* was popular. Books on church history, systematic theology, and comparative religions were common faire. I have not seen the like since. It was a job simply staying up with what the people were reading. Not that formal education was popular; rather, anything biblically oriented was of intense interest.

Murray states that there was a "sense of wonder and profound seriousness." This mark of a genuine awakening was less obvious in the JPM. The Jesus People were generally carefree—not lazy—but more inclined to the enjoyment of life than achieving the standard goals of the middle class. However, there was a great concern for spiritual things and living a life pleasing to God. For the most part, the Jesus People would settle down, throw out the marijuana and the love beads, and begin to make a life for themselves. They began to start families and accumulate to themselves those things necessary for that enterprise.

Murray's fifth point is that the same work of God would be evident in many places at once. As I pointed out earlier, there were no known *starters* of the JPM. Later accounts of the movement cite a number of different people as being instrumental in certain areas, but this was not so in the earliest part of the movement. The same things were happening in many different places, and the only possible cross-pollination would have come from the Holy Spirit. After a while, efforts were made to coordinate evangelistic meetings, conferences, retreats, and leadership gatherings. This occurred just prior to the ending of the JPM, and I believe was one of the reasons for the cessation of the awakening. By in large, the meeting of the "tribes" (tribes—a hippie orientation) were a waste of time and energy and did little to facilitate the preaching of the gospel to the unconverted. Some organization was accomplished, but disputes arose, and the most powerful, older leaders came to dominate and distort.

"Joyful praise and readiness to witness" is next on Murray's list. Nothing could better describe the JPM than joyful praise and a readiness to witness. Every meeting would end up in some kind of worshipful praise. And this is not the kind of praise celebration that is seen in either the Toronto Blessing or is commonly observed in seeker churches and churches given over to the church growth movement. For years it was usually simple singing to guitar music, happy and pleasant, soulful and loving. Later, as charismatic and pentecostal influences were seen, the praise became something quite different, but few of us saw the real difference and just accepted the new "spirit-led" format as better. Regarding witness, no one had to teach Jesus People to share their faith. Rather, leaders more often needed to teach kids more appropriate and less offensive ways to witness.

"A new energy in practical Christian service" is the seventh mark. The Jesus People seemed drawn to caring for the poor, especially for those who were homeless. The Christian houses or communes were generally open to almost anyone, and there was rarely any up-front money necessary to move in. Jesus People who had been involved with drugs desired to help prevent others from starting drugs in the first place or would urge them to turn away from drugs. Untold numbers of America's youth rejected drugs as the result of the witness of Jesus People. I personally led a Jesus People music (rock) group for four years, and our focus was drug abuse assemblies in high schools. Some of the more adventurous kids would travel the world spreading the gospel, some joined missionary groups, and some even started missionary organizations.

The eighth mark is "the recovery of family worship and family religion." This mark is more difficult to assess than the others, since most of the Jesus People, at least early on, were single. However, over time there was a reuniting with families. Due to teenage rebellion, drug use, and running away from home, many families had been divided. The JPM saw thousands of kids reunited with and reconciled to their families. One of my favorite things to do was to put a kid on a bus headed for back home. The primary point that Murray makes, however, is that a true awakening saw Christian worship in the home and not only in the Christian assembly. This was certainly the case in the JPM. Worship, praise, prayer, singing, teaching, preaching, and study of the Scripture was daily and wherever.

Lastly, Murray cites "an observable raising of the whole moral tone of society." No statistical analysis is available that might reveal the result of thousands of kids returning home and making peace with their parents. Kids touched by God in the JPM not only went back home, but they went to college, got jobs, married and started families, joined the military, and became full time workers in Christian ministry. It is not possible to imagine what would have become of the American middle class had thousands, maybe hundreds of thousands, of kids not turned away from the occult, drugs, free sex, and the gypsy life due to the JPM. We can never know for sure, but we can guess.

Beardsley's marks

Frank Beardsley, in *History of American Revivals*, gives substantially the following marks of the revival in speaking of the first great awakening: (1) there was an interest in eternal things; (2) conversations centered on theological themes; (3) the world began to hold less interest; (4) people pressed into the kingdom of God; (5) many conversions now followed; (6) this same pattern spread to surrounding towns; and (7) the revival or awakening sprang up independently in various areas.

To avoid extensive reiterations of the material given under the discussions of the marks of an awakening by Murray above, only those features given by Beardsley that differ from Murray will be discussed in any length:

People did want to hear of Jesus and the new birth; kids and adults who had merely heard about what was going on came in considerable numbers to the Jesus People gatherings. My house was often filled with people wanting to hear about Jesus. There were many conversions; the exact number will probably never be known, but because the JPM was nationwide and spread to Canada, the UK, and other places, the number of converts was probably quite large, even into the high hundreds of thousands. As before stated, the same forms we experienced in the San Francisco Bay Area appeared all over the country, and it seemed to occur of itself without organizations or dominant leaders to do the coordinating.

Beardsley's first two marks of revival are that there was an interest in eternal things and that conversations centered on theological themes. The Jesus People gradually abandoned a preoccupation with drugs, sex, politics (mainly anti-Vietnam War concerns), and counter-culture lifestyles, in favor of biblical themes and salvation. A day well spent was one where the teachings of Jesus were considered. The Bible was a constant source of interest. Scheduled Bible studies would last for hours, and there were some who wanted to stay on and on.

JPM converts would show up at any time of the day or night to talk about Jesus. The designation Jesus People is an apt one, since Jesus was the focus. The discussions were not debates and argumentation, and there was an almost uncritical hearing of biblical doctrines and themes. This is one of the reasons a number of fringe groups were able to make converts from among the Jesus People, and why several cultic, aberrant groups had their beginnings amongst them as well.

"The world began to hold less interest," is Beardsley's third mark. Some Jesus People needed to be exhorted into living productive lives. Now that Jesus had saved them and given them a new reason to live, daily working life did not seem palatable. This kind of thinking was generally temporary and perhaps necessary for many, but proper transitions did emerge.

Jonathan Edwards, in his *A Narrative of the Surprising Work of God in Northampton, Mass, 1735,* gives the following indications of a genuine spiritual awakening: (1) people earnestly discussed eternal things; (2) concern for salvation; and (3) converted people were renewed.

Edwards' list is certainly met in the JPM. While the graphic portrayals of people under strong conviction of the Holy Spirit, in terms of judgment and hell, were not generally characteristic of the JPM, in some cases it was so, and some people were terribly fearful that they would be judged and be sentenced to an everlasting hell. Though they had rejected such doctrines if they had previously known of them, many had hell and judgment strongly impressed on their minds. Perhaps it was the result of LSD or other hallucinogens, but many were relieved when they trusted in Jesus and experienced a forgiveness of sin. That which comes the closest for me in meeting the mark of accounts of conversions from the first great awakening is the centrality of Jesus for the Jesus People. Peter's statement in Acts 4:12, "Salvation is found in no one else, for there is no other name under heaven given to men by which we must be saved," could easily be the signature statement of the JPM. "One Way" was the cry, the affirmation, and the creed. With the index finger pointing straight up, the signal was given that Jesus is the only way, the only one by whom we must be saved. And this came from people who had often rejected Christianity in favor of Buddhism or Hinduism as it was taught and practiced in the hippie counter-culture.

Renewed lives were also characteristic of those who were converted in the JPM. The renewal was often dramatic. Parents, school administrators, and probation officers, among others, would often be dumbfounded at the change in not only appearance but in life direction. I think now of a young man who was so beaten down by the hippie life that he could barely speak, and whose face was obscured by a tangled mass of beard and hair, who is now a competent and successful medical doctor. I think of another young man who is a pastor of a large and healthy church in the southwest who, due to drugs, spent part of his late teen years in a mental hospital. I think of a woman who was a hippie prostitute in the Haight-Ashbury, working for money to buy heroin. After weeks of witnessing to her, she suddenly stopped me on the street one day and said she loved Jesus. She left the street that day and did not experience one bit of withdrawal from a sizeable heroin habit. (This story came to mind since she called me just recently. She is still clean and trusting in Jesus.) It would be possible for me to relate perhaps one hundred or more such stories.

Edwards' marks

C.C. Caen, editor of *The Great Awakening*, lists Edwards' five "luminous signs that a revival is of God":

> (1) It raises people's esteem of Jesus as Son of God and Savior of the world; (2) It leads them to turn away from sin and toward holiness; (3) It increases their love for the Bible; (4) It grounds them in the basic truths of the faith; and (5) It works greater love for and service to God and other people.[52]

This list of Edwards' "luminous signs that a revival is of God" is presented, because it illustrates Edwards' thinking after looking back on the awakening of which he was very much a part, and are therefore the product of some considerable experience and reflection.

Not only was Jesus lifted up in the lives of the Jesus People, but due to media coverage, Jesus and the Bible became popular across the country. Though the Jesus People might have become known in some quarters as Jesus Freaks, it had been a long while since the name of Jesus was being widely dis-

---
52   C. C. Caen, ed., *The Great Awakening* (New haven, CT: The Yale University Press, 1972), 228-248.

cussed both publicly and privately. And for the Jesus People, Jesus was the savior, the only savior.

I can testify that the genuinely converted Jesus person did turn away from sin. I flushed a lot of their drugs down my toilet, and many decks of Tarot cards, astrology charts, talismans, charms, and occult books were handed to me for disposal. Numerous were the bongs, dope pipes, hypodermic needle outfits, and other drug paraphernalia that were given up. People who considered having sex with anyone at all, as casually as eating a meal, repented and sought to live moral, sometimes celibate lives.

The Jesus People's love for the Bible has been adequately noted above. It may have been faddish for some, but many persons with whom I am still in contact yet cherish their time with the Scripture.

The fourth point is more problematic—the grounding in the basic truths of the faith. In some ways, this is difficult to assess. Some did wander into cults with strange doctrines; some of these realized the deception and escaped from those groups. Most Christian doctrines were brand new to the Jesus People, but some who were converted during that period did come from families with a history of involvement in the church, so their conversion led to more of a re-embracing of basic biblical truth.

Conclusion

It is my position that the JPM meets the marks of a genuine spiritual revival or awakening as outlined by Murray, Beardsley, and Edwards. (Many others have drawn up and deduced signs or marks of genuine revival, but the main points outlined by Murray, Beardsley, and Edwards are characteristic of most writers.) And like every genuine revival or awakening, the ending of the sovereign moving of God may open the door to human efforts to exploit or continue the awakening. This point may be illustrated by the all-night prayer meetings we conducted during the waning period of the JPM.

In late 1972 or early 1973, the church of which I was pastor instituted several all-night prayer meetings as we began to be aware, however imperfectly, of the lack of spiritual power and success in ministry that had settled upon us. It was our conviction that if we put "sin out of the camp," continued steadfastly in prayer (and fasting), and did all else that we could—revival would come. We had learned this from Charles Finney's *Revival Lectures,* which we used as a guide for our evangelism. We thought that if we did what was required, then God would move in power. At that point in my life I had no idea that God was the one who brought awakening, though I would have readily admitted to the fact that God is sovereign.

Perhaps a primary motivation for the church growth movement, at least early on, was to see the continuation of the obvious outpouring of the Spirit that characterized the JPM. Many of the leaders of this movement were involved in the JPM, usually in the latter stages of it, and wanted to see God do great things. The problem was that they did not understand the nature of an awakening and the sovereignty of God. Despite the aberrations, the JPM yet stands as a true awakening. As it seems with each genuine move of the Spirit of God, this one also has its dark side, its wild fire.

In the present times, when there is no awakening apparent, we are not discouraged or disillusioned—indeed a mighty wind of the Spirit may blow tomorrow and sweep great numbers into the kingdom of God. Yes, I would love to see this once more in my lifetime. Whether I am privileged to see something that would so greatly glorify our God and Savior Jesus Christ as the JPM again, I do not know, but I know I saw it once, and for that I am grateful.

Five:
The last awakening (?-?)

Will America experience another awakening?

American Christians may ask God to pour out his Holy Spirit to both revive his Church and sweep into that Church those whom he will. These prayers will be numbered in the many thousands, but they will not force God into acting. He will act according to his good pleasure.

American Christians will preach for revival and awakening, preach the grand story we call the gospel, including law and grace, and depend upon God to work his miracle of renewal and new birth. But such preaching will not force his hand.

American Christians will plan for revival and awakening, and those plans will not be taken to be magical manipulations, as though we could determine what God will do; but even the most righteous biblical planning will not achieve much, unless his divine strategy is worked out.

For some time I have cherished a desire to be a street Christian again engaged in personal evangelism, even of a confrontational nature, distributing evangelistically oriented literature, fearlessly street preaching with the simple gospel as the only content—part of an army of zealous Christians, of many backgrounds and identifications, day in and day out hitting the highways and byways across America with a message of law, love, and grace, the central defining elements of the gospel. Yes, I would dearly love to be so engaged, and maybe I will do it one day, not as a young hippie following Jesus but as a mature adult, intent on fulfilling the great commission. And still, if this were all realized, and though there be those who would turn from sin to Jesus, an awakening as described in this book would not necessarily arise.

Will America see normal times set aside and experience another awakening? My view is this: if America does not see another awakening like those described in this book, or on the contrary, if America does see a hundred more great awakenings in the years to come, I think there will be at least one other and final great awakening.

Normal and awakening times

An important lesson for me was understanding the difference between "normal" and "awakening" times. In normal times we pray, preach, and plan for awakening, and in the process some Christians are spiritually renewed and there are some conversions. But this is not like times of awakening, when the Spirit of God is poured out in ways that are not customary in normal times. Normal is what we usually experience; awakenings are rare. Awakenings come suddenly, and then they go. We do not understand it at all, and we do not control it at all; it all belongs to the sovereign will of God.

Awakenings are going on somewhere most of the time

In America right now we are not experiencing revival, at least not on a national scale. However, across America—in small towns, in large or small churches, maybe in a home or at an office—awakenings could be taking place. We notice the large ones but not the small ones. Around the world, awakenings are taking place right now—some large, some small. God is working still and will until the end of the age.

Without qualms I make this assessment because of the information that comes to me daily—news of Christians at work and witness all over the world. Though I do not notice any exceptionally large awakenings happening this moment, except in parts of Africa, it seems likely that there are many small ones going on, even right now. Some of these are in countries dominated by Islam, or Hinduism, even Buddhism. There is encouraging news coming out of Mexico and out of Central and South America. We have also heard of the wonderful events taking place in parts of Asia and Africa, and even in the Jewish homeland. Globally speaking, we are in the midst of awakenings.

It may be that what we have seen in the past and observe in the present will be eclipsed by something even larger in the future.

The last great awakening

There is an entity that may play a very large role in the unwinding of the age. That entity is the nation Israel. Some readers may be disheartened by my bringing up this subject, while others may readily agree with my viewpoint.

My theology is most closely akin to the Reformed tradition, though for much of my Christian life I embraced Arminian/Dispensational theology. After moving to a Calvinistic or Reformed theology, I have had difficulty with the place of Israel in the end times, because I found that so many Calvinists embraced variations of what is generally termed Replacement Theology. Essentially, this means that the Church replaces Israel in terms of God's grand promises to Israel found in the Old Testament. My research into the matter did not solve the problem, and my thinking remained divided on the issue. However, after recently teaching through Romans, as I explained in the preface, I began to change my view. This view is my own, how I see things right now, and I know there are many biblically faithful commentators who have concluded otherwise. Perhaps my hermeneutics are based on my desire to see another great awakening like I saw firsthand in the

Jesus People Movement—that is for others to decide, but let me briefly present my case.

Israel and the last great awakening

At my side is a stack of books a foot or so high. These are commentaries on Romans and other general books on systematic theology. The authors are dispensational, Reformed, and "other" in opinion, and I had thought that I would present the opinions expressed as clearly as I could. Then I thought better of it. After all, I would only be expressing opinions and viewpoints of some very fine scholars, none of whom could be declared to be inspired and without error. Instead, I will make a case for my viewpoint only and let readers ferret it out for themselves. Whether one disagrees with my opinion or not, I hope it would not detract from the book overall.

Below are two passages written by the Apostle Paul to the Church in Rome, which occupy a large place concerning the question at hand:

> So I ask, did they stumble in order that they might fall? By no means! Rather through their trespass salvation has come to the Gentiles, so as to make Israel jealous. Now if their trespass means riches for the world, and if their failure means riches for the Gentiles, how much more will their full inclusion mean! Romans 11:11-12

> Lest you be wise in your own conceits, I want you to understand this mystery, brothers: a partial hardening has come upon Israel, until the fullness of the Gentiles has come in. And in this way all Israel will be saved, as it is written, "The Deliverer will come from Zion, he will banish ungodliness from Jacob"; "and this will be my

covenant with them when I take away their sins."
Romans 11:25-27

A question asked for centuries is, What constitutes Israel? Is it national identity, race, culture, ethnicity, geography, religion, genetics, or something else? This will be debated as long as the planet survives. God knows who Israel is, and we can let it go at that, yet I think that the "Church" is not Israel in Romans 11:11-12. Paul contrasts Gentiles and Israel in this passage. Here he is not speaking of Israel as the Church or the other way around. Israel is distinct; it is the nation, or at least the remnant chosen by grace. Something Paul taught earlier in the Roman letter must be kept in mind: "For not all who are descended from Israel belong to Israel" (Romans 9:6). Israel is the "People of God" and is a remnant or part of the larger nation of Israel.

In Romans 11:25-27 Paul makes the same distinction between Israel and Gentile Christians. Paul then quotes two passages, Isaiah 59:20-21 and Isaiah 27:9, to affirm that first, the Messiah will come from Israel and second, the sins of Jacob (or Israel) will be removed. In other words, the atoning work of Messiah Jesus will impact Israel at a future point in time. While the prophecies of Isaiah could easily be understood as referring to the Church built by Jesus, by Paul's era that Church was fully established. Paul then, it seems to me, has a forward historical event in mind.

Jesus points to a future saving event for Jerusalem

Immediately prior to Jesus' foretelling of the destruction of the temple and the describing of the signs of the end of the age, Matthew's Gospel places his lament over Jerusalem:

> "O Jerusalem, Jerusalem, the city that kills the prophets and stones those who are sent to it! How often would I have gathered your

children together as a hen gathers her brood under her wings, and you would not! See, your house is left to you desolate. For I tell you, you will not see me again, until you say, 'Blessed is he who comes in the name of the Lord.'"
Matthew 23:37-39

Our passage comes at the conclusion of the seven "woes" directed at the religious leaders of Israel. Though Jesus' words seem harsh they may instead be an effort to reach out to those who had hardened their hearts against him. At the close of his ministry, Jesus finds one more opportunity to break through the darkness of unbelief.

"Jerusalem"—this would likely indicate the nation of Israel itself and not merely the inhabitants of the city alone. Jesus expresses sadness and lament over the fate of his own kin and country due to their rejection of his Messiahship. Included in that fate was desolation, the destruction of the city and temple through the agency of the Roman general Titus in A.D. 70.

Yet there is a ray of hope in Jesus' lament, and it is in the single word "until." There is a hope of a future time when the fortunes of Jerusalem, or Israel, would be dramatically altered. And when that moment occurred, Jerusalem would shout out again, "'Blessed is he who comes in the name of the Lord'" (Matthew 23:39 and Matthew 21:10). Yes, two passages with identical wording are found in Matthew; the second was uttered by those who welcomed Jesus into Jerusalem at the event we know as the Triumphal Entry.

My view is that Jesus will hear Israel, whatever Israel is, once again shout the words of the Hallel Psalm 118:26, the song of the pilgrims on their way to the great feast, perhaps the Feast of Tabernacles, the final ingathering. And this may be the time when Israel looks upon him whom they pierced (see Zechariah 12:10).

All Israel will be saved

Certainly, there has been a remnant from Israel in the Church all along. The early church was all Jewish at one point, then less Jewish, until Jews became a minority within the Church. But they were still there and are here to this day.

Whoever and whatever Israel is, it will be saved. And this will be at a future time in history, at a point that looks like the final event of history—a last great awakening.

Israel—the elect from within that nation, the rescued of the remnant alive at the end of human history? Israel—the nation itself? Israel—those who consider themselves Jewish? Israel—those with DNA that biologically links to Abraham and Sarah? Israel—those observant Jews yet seeking to obey the Law? Israel—Jews looking for the coming of the Messiah? Israel—the Church made up of Jews and Gentiles? This last one is held by many Reformed Christians, but if that is correct, does it negate that there will be one last great awakening?

Though I do not understand it all, my thinking is that God's Israel does play a role in the end times and that there will be a great awakening, an abundant outpouring of grace upon that Israel.

When Israel is saved, it will be through Jesus Christ and he alone—there will not be a separate or different way in which Israel will be saved. To be clear, Jews will not have salvation simply because they are Jews. Here the Reformed doctrine of election makes perfect sense. Israel will be called, justified, and glorified in the very same way any of God's elect are saved. God will do it according to his good pleasure. And Israel will not be converted without the agency of preaching, and that preaching may be very diverse in method, but it will be by preaching, just as Paul had already declared, "So faith comes from hearing, and hearing through the word of Christ" (Romans 10:17).

Do we have a part?

It is fitting and right to pray for revival and awakening; in fact, it is our duty to do so. May we make David's plea our own when he said, "Pray for the peace of Jerusalem" (Psalm 122:6). Jesus is the peace of Jerusalem, the peace or salvation he secured through his death and resurrection. Could it be that the words of Zechariah 12:10, describing a spirit of repentance coming upon Israel, will be fulfilled in the final awakening?

> "And I will pour out on the house of David
> and the inhabitants of Jerusalem
> a spirit of grace and pleas for mercy,
> so that, when they look on me,
> on him whom they have pierced,
> they shall mourn for him, as one mourns
> for an only child, and weep bitterly over him,
> as one weeps over a firstborn."

Appendix A:
A summary of Jonathan Edwards' Distinguishing marks of the work of the Spirit of God

Author's introduction

In 1741 Jonathan Edwards wrote *Distinguishing marks of the work of the Spirit of God*[53] to defend what he considered to be the work of the Spirit of God and convince those who disagreed.

In 1727 Edwards was called to the Congregational Church at Northampton, Massachusetts, to serve under his grandfather Solomon Stoddard, who was then in the fifty-eighth year of his pastorate. In 1729 Stoddard died and Edwards was installed as pastor of the church. Due to a number of factors, chief among them the impact of the "Half-way Covenant," many of Edwards' congregation were unconverted. In 1735, or just earlier than this, Edwards observed the circumstance and set about in his preaching to meet this great need. Slowly some were converted, then more and more. The number ran, or so Edwards thought, to finally reach about 300. This was nearly a quarter of the inhabitants of the entire town of Northampton.

Edwards was a careful and diligent pastor of his people, visiting them regularly and interviewing all who were being "wrought upon" by the Spirit. He was no enthusiast or reviv-

---
53 *Distinguishing Marks of a Work of the Spirit of God* may be found at: http://www.biblebb.com/files/edwards/je-marksofhs.htm.

alist; he was as meticulous in his observations of people as he was of the flora and fauna around him. (Edwards may be considered the first biologist in America.) In addition, he observed the spiritual condition of the members of the church from 1727 to 1741, the year he wrote the book now under consideration. Northampton was a small town, and nothing much would have been missed by the thoughtful and reflective Edwards. He also had some knowledge of previous "harvests" in Northampton, five of these during the ministry of his grandfather. Edwards then had some experience, though via his grandfather, of the way in which God had worked to bring salvation to others in that very same region of western Massachusetts.

In all of Edwards' writings he was careful to examine psychological elements involved in the processes of religion. Some have said that Edwards, in addition to being America's finest theologian, was America's first psychologist. Therefore, his analysis of the working of the Spirit of God cannot be easily dismissed.

Though I have become somewhat accustomed to Edwards style and syntax, he is nevertheless difficult for many to read. I have thought it helpful to highlight some of Edwards' chief points, and greatly shorten, even summarize, Edwards' evaluation so that more students of awakenings might benefit. In a few places I have inserted opinions of my own. It is the hope and prayer of Christians of all ages that God will continue to awaken and revive, and to that end we desire to recognize and appreciate those momentous times.

In italics with brackets, I comment on how Edwards' material relates to my experience of the JPM.

If possible, I would apologize to Jonathan Edwards for this reworking, knowing I could never come close to the exacting yet beautiful rendering of the awesome work God did through his ministry in Northampton, Massachusetts.

Summary or brief outline of Distinguishing Marks of a Work of the Spirit of God

Edward's untitled introduction

"Beloved, believe not every spirit, but try the spirits whether they are of God; because many false prophets are gone out into the world" (1 John 4:1). This verse sits at the head of the book and was the first verse in Edwards' chief text, 1 John 4:1-12.

Edwards's introduction begins with:

> In the apostolic age, there was the greatest outpouring of the Spirit of God that ever was; both as to his extraordinary influences and gifts, and his ordinary operations, in convincing, converting, enlightening, and sanctifying the souls of men. But as the influences of the true Spirit abounded, so counterfeits did also abound: the devil was abundant in mimicking, both the ordinary and extraordinary influences of the Spirit of God, as is manifest by innumerable passages of the apostles' writings.

He brings out certain points in 1 John 4 that are apostolic marks of a genuine work of the Spirit of God. There will be counterfeits because of the work of false prophets, who closely resemble true preachers of the gospel. Edwards states his goal thus:

> My design therefore at this time is to show what are the true, certain, and distinguishing evidences of a work of the Spirit of God, by which we may safely proceed in judging of any operation we find in ourselves, or see in others.

[If leaders of the JPM had been exposed to Edwards' views, many errors and distortions may well have been avoided. I, for one, would have benefited. We tended to have a naïve view of the events happening around and to us, and if it was spiritual, or even emotionally based, we simply assumed it was of God. This was more true of the earlier years of the JPM, but by at least 1970, many of us were aware of counterfeits, such as the Children of God and The Way International.]

Section A

Negative Signs; or, What are no signs by which we are to judge of a work—and especially, What are no evidences that a work is not from the Spirit of God.

This introduces a section of material that is the most difficult for me to summarize, and it contains some ideas of which I am unsure. His primary point is that because something is different or unusual, both in terms of the Scripture or previous experience, that does not necessarily mean it cannot be a work of the Spirit. Edwards says,

> The Holy Spirit is sovereign in his operation; and we know that he uses a great variety; and we cannot tell how great a variety he may use, within the compass of the rules he himself has fixed.

[This argument has been used by proponents of what has been called The Laughing Revival, or The Toronto Blessing, or The River. Leaders would warn that though what is observed is unusual, that alone does not disqualify it from being a work of God. I doubt Edwards would have agreed, because the behaviors he observed are not even close to what was defended in the above-mentioned so-called revivals. In fact, Edwards did ques-

tion some bizarre aspects of the awakening, sometimes without coming to definite conclusions about them.]

I. Therefore it is not reasonable to determine that a work is not from God's Holy Spirit because of the extraordinary degree in which the minds of persons are influenced.

Here Edwards is referring to the impact of preaching. Law and grace were preached most strongly, and people would come under powerful conviction of their sin, even to the point of being fearful of falling into hell itself. Some would fall to the ground under the pressure of genuine conviction from the Holy Spirit. It was only the preaching that produced this and not efforts to create a highly emotional state of mind. Indeed, much of the preaching produced dramatic reactions in the hearers, especially under the preaching of George Whitefield and Edwards himself. Edwards argues that such convicting work of the Spirit, though not common, is no reason to suspect it is merely an emotional or psychological phenomenon. Edwards uses the example of the first outpouring at Pentecost in Acts 2. He says,

> The great unusualness of the work surprised the Jews; they knew not what to make of it, but could not believe it to be the work of God: many looked upon the persons that were the subjects of it as bereft of reason.

[In the JPM, the power of the converting work of the Spirit was equally surprising. To see people struggle with the convicting work of the Spirit through preaching or personal witness was sometimes frightening. It was not business as usual, as I could plainly see when I compared my experiences in the JPM with my pastorate in Byron, California. And the joy that would be expressed by people who found peace in Jesus was something

I actually attempted, at times, to repress. It took me awhile to learn that some praise and shouting for joy was not error or excessive. I found that people trapped in sin and confusion, dread and fear, would not hesitate to express their deliverance in robust ways.]

II. A work is not to be judged by any effects on the bodies of men; such as tears, trembling, groans, loud outcries, agonies of body, or the failing of bodily strength.

Edwards, like Paul in Scripture, examines things very closely and will cover a topic very thoroughly, so much so that it may seem that the points are redundant. Here again Edwards is saying that emotions such as tears, groans, and loud outcries should be expected, given the makeup of humankind when a convicted sinner experiences the powerful working of the Spirit of God. He wrote:

> There are none of us but do suppose, and would have been ready at any time to say it, that the misery of hell is doubtless so dreadful, and eternity so vast, that if a person should have a clear apprehension of that misery as it is, it would be more than his feeble frame could bear, and especially if at the same time he saw himself in great danger of it.

This description shows Edwards' connecting human behavior and biblical doctrine. But he did understand the areas where there was no explicit Scripture warrant.

> I do not know that we have any express mention in the New Testament of any person's weeping, or groaning, or sighing through fear of hell, or a sense of God's anger; but is there

anybody so foolish as from hence to argue, that in whomsoever these things appear, their convictions are not from the Spirit of God?

Some of what Edwards saw was unusual, but nevertheless it was only what one might expect, and that the Scripture does not speak directly to a particular issue does not mean Scripture would be opposed.

III. It is no argument that an operation on the minds of people is not the work of the Spirit of God, that it occasions a great deal of noise about religion.

That the apostles turned the world upside down was probably not done quietly (see Acts17:6), but it would be expected that there would be some commotion or noise. Edward's protested:

> And when was there ever any such thing since the world stood, as a people in general being greatly affected in any affair whatsoever, without noise or stir? The nature of man will not allow it.

[Edwards point, from my view, is well taken. That many in the JPM were noisy is certainly true. However, I was involved in the Catholic Charismatic Movement that emerged prior to the JPM. In addition, I was much acquainted with, and spoke at early men's and women's Charismatic gatherings. At times these gatherings, in my opinion, would get strange and unusual. Certainly, there were some elements of excessive behavior during the JPM, especially with those groups that emphasized healing and the so-called "prophetic words." These meetings appeared later in the JPM and would alarm me. In these meetings, the gospel was not the focus of the preaching.]

IV. It is no argument that an operation on the minds of a people is not the work of the Spirit of God, that many who are the subjects of it, have great impressions made on their imaginations.

By "impressions" Edwards is referring to people's sense that God is speaking to or revealing things to them. His point was that God's work of conviction of sin followed by the peace that comes with forgiveness and salvation will have an impact on the minds and emotions of those so affected. And most Christians will say "amen" to that.

Detractors were saying that there was little real religion in the awakening; it was simply emotionally-based "impressions." Edwards thought that "affections" would be experienced in real and vital religious experiences, must be so, or there would be little evidence to say that anything like a saving event had occurred. He wrote:

> It is no argument that a work is not of the Spirit of God, that some who are the subjects of it have been in a kind of ecstasy, wherein they have been carried beyond themselves, and have had their minds transported into a train of strong and pleasing imaginations, and a kind of visions, as though they were rapt up even to heaven, and there saw glorious sights. I have been acquainted with some such instances, and I see no need of bringing in the help of the devil into the account that we give of these things, nor yet of supposing them to be of the same nature with the visions of the prophets, or St. Paul's rapture in paradise.

Edwards' wife was given to impressions at times so that he was able to observe these things up close. Though he saw that there could be excesses, it was to be expected that the work of God in conversion would produce, must produce, effects on both body and mind. Some detractors charged it was the devil as well as the emotions that were involved. Edwards, based on his experience, was certain the devil must not be so credited.

Unlike biblical visions, people imagined themselves to have been swept up into heaven in the joy of their salvation—Edwards thought it was all within the normal range of human experience. He saw that these did not last but were temporary. Christian literature, in addition, is replete with the same. And when certain people gave too much weight to the visions and revelations they thought came from God, as time passed and nothing came of it, that was simply the end of it.

[It was very typical of many in the JPM that they would imagine themselves to be given visions and revelations. This was more the case in the JPM than in the first awakening because of the close link with charismatic and Pentecostal influences. At times it was a real problem and created some difficulty for me. Learning how to be discerning of spiritual experiences was a frequent subject of Bible studies and sermons. Even at the worst of times, the ecstasies passed on and little damage was done. However, some people would be carried away by a strong personality who claimed so-called power gifts, like prophesy and healing. Most troubling were those who claimed to have discovered what actual New Testament Christianity should look like.

Outpourings of the Spirit of God seem to be tainted with such distortions. Whether from the human spirit gone awry or from an unclean spirit, these still do not lead to the conclusion that the overall JPM was not a work of the Spirit of God. A negative judgment of a work of the Spirit must not depend upon the aberrations and delusions of some.]

V. It is no sign that a work is not from the Spirit of God, that example is a great means of it.

By "example" Edwards meant that the awakening spread through contact with others who had experienced awakenings. Old Lights criticized that the awakening used "means" and was then not genuine; one of the "means" was by "example."

Edwards argued that such a means as *example* was indeed observed in the awakening, but that did not mean the awakening was not a work of God. In other words, the awakening was spread by the Spirit of God and it was not a case of copying or imitation. He said, "Example is one of God's means; and certainly it is no argument that a work is not of God, that his own means are made use of to affect it." He goes on to say, "There never yet was a time of remarkable pouring out of the Spirit, and great revival of religion, but that example had a main hand." He mentions the reformation and the cross fertilization that took place to carry the reformation to most of northern Europe, and he further notes that the biblically recorded outpourings in Jerusalem, Samaria, and Ephesus had their connections. He stated:

> As in those days one person was moved by another, so one city or town was influenced by the example of another, 1 Thess. i.7, 8. "so that ye were ensamples to all that believe in Macedonia and Achaia, for from you sounded out the word of the Lord, not only in Macedonia and Achaia, but also in every place your faith to God-ward is spread abroad."

[In 1968 some of us from the San Francisco Bay Area began to travel to other parts of the country and found that what we were doing in California was being done in other places as well—street evangelism, Bible and tract distribution, the founding of small Christian communities, the creation of new forms of music, and so on. Undoubtedly there was a cross fertilization that took place, a learning from each other, but the basic forms seem to have arisen independently of outside influ-

ences. It surely was not a sociological phenomenon. We barely knew what we were doing most of the time, yet we were seeing relatively large numbers of people being converted. Usually we were dumbfounded and had to then deal with how to handle the new believers suddenly in our care.]

VI. It is no sign that a work is not from the Spirit of God, that many who seem to be the subjects of it, are guilty of great imprudences and irregularities in their conduct.

On this point, Edwards' opening paragraph is:

> We are to consider that the end for which God pours out his Spirit, is to make men holy, and not to make them politicians. It is no wonder that, in a mixed multitude of all sorts—wise and unwise, young and old, of weak and strong natural abilities, under strong impressions of mind—there are many who behave themselves imprudently.

Pastors as experienced as Edwards knew that mature Christian character and behavior was not automatic in new converts. Most Christians come to this understanding later if not sooner. Detractors used spiritual immaturity to affirm the awakening was not of God. As a Calvinist, Edwards held to the doctrine of sanctification as being a slow, steady, and sure process that went on the entire length of a Christian's life. He was not surprised when Christians behaved in unseemly ways, and he clearly understood that a person could be genuinely converted but yet have problems to work through. Non-Christians generally do not see this and are quick to point the finger and say, "Ah-ha! look at the hypocrites."

Edwards used the Corinthian church of the New Testament as an example:

> There is scarcely any church more celebrated in the New Testament for being blessed with large measures of the Spirit of God, ...yet what manifold imprudences, great and sinful irregularities, and strange confusion did they run into, at the Lord's supper, and in the exercise of church discipline!

Edwards admitted the deficiencies of some who were leaders in the awakening.

> And if we see great imprudences, and even sinful irregularities, in some who are great instruments to carry on the work, it will not prove it not to be a work of God.

Edwards cited the incident where Paul confronted Peter over the issue of Peter's withdrawal from table fellowship with Gentiles.

> If a great pillar of the Christian church—one of the chief of those who are the very foundations on which, next to Christ, the whole church is said to be built—was guilty of such an irregularity; is it any wonder if other lesser instruments, who have not that extraordinary conduct of the divine Spirit he had, should be guilty of many irregularities?

Edward's may have had in mind the criticism that was aimed at George Whitefield, George Tennent, and James Davenport by some of the Old Lights like Charles Chauncy, who bristled at the idea that some ministers, like himself, who opposed the awakenings, were being accused of being unconverted. And there were certain excesses that these preachers were guilty of and which Edwards disapproved of. Indeed, he spoke to those he considered to have crossed lines of respectability, and with good result, eventually. Edwards concluded,

> And in particular, it is no evidence that a work is not of God, if many who are either the subjects or the instrument of it, are guilty of too great forwardness to censure others as unconverted.

Certainly among the converts there would have been those who were truly converted but yet continued in behavior that was not authentically Christian, or others who had only experienced a false conversion and who also were not conforming to traditional Christian behavior, but the point is that these do not negate an actual outpouring of the Spirit of God.

[This point in particular reminds me of the detractors I faced in the JPM. Most of the converts were young people who had been convinced that the goal of life was freedom—a political, psychological, sexual, and so on. They had thought it was drugs, mainly LSD and marijuana, that were the vehicles to reach that freedom. When they then suddenly became Christians, often far from home and loaded with hormones and the desire for adventure, the results were problems for us. And most of us "elders" were barely out of that mentality ourselves. It was often almost the case of the blind leading the blind.

At this point in my history, I can see that though many struggled mightily and failed time and again, these youngsters matured and continue today to show up stable, sober, and in their right minds—and more than that, still following Jesus.]

VII. Nor are many errors in judgment, and some delusions of Satan intermixed with the work, any argument that the work in general is not of the Spirit of God.

Here Edwards takes it a step further: not only is bad behavior not a bar to the awakening being a work of God, but also it is no bar if it should be so that Satan's influence should somehow be part of it.

> Many godly persons have undoubtedly in this and other ages, exposed themselves to woeful delusions, by an aptness to lay too much weight on impulses and impressions, as if they were immediate revelations from God, to signify something future, or to direct them where to go, and what to do.

Perhaps Edwards had in mind the trouble and confusion that James Davenport brought to the awakening, of which Davenport later repented. It is not clear that Edwards was only thinking of possibilities that Satan might be involved or that he was referring to detractor's charges that Satan was really in the mix. He knew enough of Christian history to consider and accept the actual involvement of demonic counterfeits in the awakening and knew that this was no proof that the work was not of the Spirit of God.

[The JPM was undoubtedly, according to my estimation, greatly troubled by demonic influences. I think of David Berg and the Children of God or of Jim Jones of the People's Temple in San Francisco—and I had, unhappily, much experience with both.

Though the Children of God were active in the early years of 1968 to 1970, in some parts of California they seemed to be only a small irritation. The COG did harm us greatly in their taking over much of the ministry of David Hoyt; still it was nowhere near the trouble of what was called "The Shepherding Movement." That story is somewhat described in the chapter on the JPM; but Jim Jones was real trouble and close at hand.

Miracles were being reported to occur at the People's Temple. So many people from my own congregation were attending services there that I made some visits to find out for myself what was going on. Jim Jones was so bold as to send a school bus every Sunday morning to our church's parking lot to load our people up to take them to his services. This did not last too long, for I soon found a way to stop it.

And there were miracles, too—strange signs and wonders, and certainly supernatural. People could reach up and shake hands with an "angel." Oil would drop from the ceiling on open Bibles, and only on open Bibles. There were definite and strong smells of "the sweet savor of the Lord," and once I witnessed when a twelve year old black girl stood on the platform next to Jim Jones, and the stigmata appeared on her hands, feet, and side. Yes, I saw and experienced these things. No wonder Jones attracted such a crowd and had such power over those people. There were definitely signs and wonders, but they were counterfeit, like the work of the magicians of Egypt in Moses' day, but miracles nonetheless.

This section could extend many pages more; my point is that I agree with Edwards that the presence of the demonic is no reason at all to deny the genuineness of a work of the Spirit of God.]

VIII. If some, who were thought to be wrought upon, fall away into gross errors, to scandalous practices, it is no argument that the work in general is not the work of the Spirit of God.

That there are some counterfeits, is no argument that nothing is true: such things are always expected in a time of reformation. If we look into church history, we shall find no instance of any great revival of religion, but what has been attended with many such things. Instances of this nature in the apostles' days were innumerable; some fell away into gross heresies, others into vile practices, though they seemed to be subjects of a work of the Spirit—and were accepted for a while amongst those that were truly so, as their brethren and companions—and were not suspected till they went out from them.

This point does logically follow the two preceding, that people thought to be converted—and it is difficult, if not impossible, to know the truth in each case—would fall into gross theological error and scandalous behavior. Pastors regularly see this in normal times, so reason would have it that the sheer weight of numbers would produce more examples of it during times of awakening. Edwards saw it, heard of it, and knew that the awakening was not false because of errors and strange behavior. He had been around long enough to see some of those who had acted so badly reform, repent, and follow again along the narrow way.

[That colonial awakening was meek and mild in comparison to others, including the JPM, and perhaps worse was what occurred during and what followed the second awakening, out of which came some of the largest Bible-based cults.

Tragic events accompanied the JPM; many still have to cope with the excesses of it. Outweighing the negative is how many more whose names are now written in the Lamb's Book of Life. And for some of the most scandalous bad actors, that part of their lives proved to be only a snapshot in time, and another photo would tell a different, even God-glorifying story. People who had been body slammed, including me, have gotten up again, and though injured, have continued the race—with fruit, too.

My testimony mirrors so closely that of Edwards'—despite all that went wrong, still God worked in his mysterious and sovereign way.]

IX. It is no argument that a work is not from the Spirit of God, that it seems to be promoted by ministers insisting very much on the terrors of God's holy law, and that with a great deal of pathos and earnestness.

Reformed theology will emphasize that the gospel is of two parts, law and grace. It is almost like a formula: law + grace = gospel. When the law is preached it often will cause a reaction in those not assured of their cleansing from sin by the atoning blood of Jesus Christ. It is clear that the Bible teaches that only hell awaits those not washed in the blood of the Lamb. Preachers of the First Great Awakening did preach the reality of hell, and Edwards warned that the preaching must be genuine, not cold and indifferent. Edwards argues:

> If there be really a hell of such dreadful and never-ending torments, as is generally supposed, of which multitudes are in great danger—and into which the greater part of men in Christian countries do actually from generation to generation fall, for want of a sense of its terribleness, and so for want of taking due care to avoid it—then why is it not proper for those who have the care of souls to take great pains to make men sensible of it: Why should they not be told as much of the truth as can be?

Many awakening preachers, the New Lights, were not afraid of offending people by preaching law and the danger of hell for the unforgiven. These preachers were not men-pleasers nor fearful of negative reaction. All preachers will be wounded by critical reaction, of course, but compared to their duty to preach the truth, these men knew that fear of men must not deter them. Edwards said:

APPENDIX A

> The main work of ministers is to preach the gospel: Christ is the end of the law for righteousness.

And he goes so far as to say,

> Some talk of it as an unreasonable thing to fright persons to heaven; but I think it is a reasonable thing to endeavour to fright persons away from hell.

[The preaching of the reality of hell was not a major feature of the witness in the JPM, but it was not absent either. There was a constant emphasis on various sins, especially drug use and free love, but we were not as vociferous about the torments of hell as seen in the preachers of the first awakening. My own approach was to teach on the wages of sin in Bible studies, where I could field questions and deal with objections. However, heaven and hell were accepted doctrines among the Jesus People, which was often reflected in the music of that era. Some, particularly those who were involved in what was called deliverance ministry—the casting out of demons—well knew the awful truth about the devil and his angels as well as their abode.]

Section B

What are distinguishing scripture evidences of a work of the Spirit of God.

Edwards begins his second section with:

> Having shown, in some instances, what are not evidences that a work wrought among a people, is not a work of the Spirit of God, I now proceed, in the second place, as was proposed, to show positively, what are the sure, distinguishing scripture evidences and marks of a work of the Spirit of God, by which we may proceed in judging of any operation we find in ourselves, or see among a people, without danger of being misled.—And in this, as I said before, I shall confine myself wholly to those marks which are given us by the apostle in the chapter wherein is my text, where this matter is particularly handled, and more plainly and fully than anywhere else in the Bible. And in speaking of these marks, I shall take them in the order in which I find them in the chapter.

I. When the operation is such as to raise their esteem of that Jesus who was born of the Virgin, and was crucified without the gates of Jerusalem; and seems more to confirm and establish their minds in the truth of what the gospel declares to us of his being the Son of God, and the Saviour of men; is a sure sign that it is from the Spirit of God.

The awakening preachers lifted up the person and work of Jesus Christ. Their sermons were full of Jesus, the Jesus of the Bible and of the accepted creeds of the historic Church.

Though Deism was flourishing, the Jesus they presented—teacher, humanitarian, or illumined prophet—was not the Jesus preached by Whitefield, Davies, the Tennents, or Edwards. Edwards made it clear that the awakening preacher's doctrine of Christ was orthodox and apostolic. Those who were then converted held Jesus in high esteem, which was a marked difference from their previous evaluation.

The devil, Edwards points out, would never lift up Jesus but would rather deny him and his work of salvation. But the awakening brought an undeniable focus on the great work of God in Christ.

[The JPM focused on the person of Jesus Christ; Jesus was at the center of it all, and those who had little interest in him prior to conversion saw all that change, radically so. It was Jesus the God-man, Lord and Savior, dying, rising from the dead, ready to return for his Bride, who was proclaimed long and loud. This was especially true for many years. The emphasis on the Holy Spirit, due to the impact of the Charismatic Movement during the 1970s, did become a major focus. Spiritual gifts, especially speaking in tongues, prophecy, and "singing in the Spirit" received far too much attention while gospel preaching and Bible teaching seemed to decrease. This was not true for the entirety of the Jesus People, only for those who had embraced the Charismatic Movement, like I had.]

II When the spirit that is at work operates against the interests of Satan's kingdom, which lies in encouraging and establishing sin, and cherishing men's worldly lusts; this is a sure sign that it is a true, and not a false spirit.

Edwards had a biblical view of Satan and the demonic kingdom. Edwards knew a true work of God did not advance the interests of Satan. This point follows closely to and logically from the point above—they are inseparable. Satan would not, as was normal in the awakening, convince men of sin and awaken the conscience about the consequences thereof. No, this can only be the work of the Holy Spirit.

> So that we may safely determine, from what the apostle says, that the spirit that is at work amongst a people, after such a manner, as to lessen men's esteem of the pleasures, profits, and honours of the world, and to take off their hearts from an eager pursuit after these things; and to engage them in a deep concern about a future state and eternal happiness which the gospel reveals—and puts them upon earnestly seeking the kingdom of God and his righteousness; and the spirit that convinces them of the dreadfulness of sin, the guilt it brings, and the misery to which it exposes; must needs be the Spirit of God.

[A large number of those who were converted in the JPM came out of the hippie life, or were influenced by it, which was characterized by drug use and casual sex. It did take a powerful work of the Holy Spirit to turn such people away from cheap and easy sinning to a holy and righteous God. But that is what happened, and the contrast observed in the lives of the Jesus People was very large and clear.]

III. The spirit that operates in such a manner, as to cause in men a greater regard to the Holy Scriptures, and establishes them more in their truth and divinity, is certainly the Spirit of God.

Edwards' point is based on 1 John 4:6—true believers will listen to the words of the apostles. Those converted in the awakening, Edwards could plainly observe, developed a love for the Bible and spent much time in it. Certainly, Edwards knew that the devil never would attempt to beget in persons a regard to that divine word which God has given to be the great and standing rule for the direction of his church.

The high regard for Scripture then was a sure sign of the Spirit of God.

[The Bible figured large in the lives of the Jesus People. The most attended meetings were the Bible studies. High school kids carried big black Bibles to school with them. I saw lunch time Bible studies in class rooms that could hardly contain the crowds of kids who wanted to be included. It was in the JPM that I developed my verse-by-verse studies—no notes, no other books, just the Word, and people would sit for hours reading and studying the Bible. Some of the ex-hippies, those who thought they would find reality in LSD, became almost too attached to their Bibles and would cause me to worry that they were becoming obsessed. Usually it was only a short time before they would return to a more balanced concern for the Scripture. Here it was—the very Word of God and they/we could not get enough.]

IV. Another rule to judge of spirits may be drawn from those compellations given to the opposite spirits, in the last words of the 6th verse, "The spirit of truth and the spirit of error."

The spirit of truth will lead to truth, and once that truth is held to and embraced, it will lead away from counterfeits of the truth. The truth brings people into the light, and the light exposes the darkness and those things of darkness. Edwards said,

> If we observe that the spirit at work makes men more sensible than they used to be, that there is a God, and that he is a great and sin-hating God; that life is short, and very uncertain; and that there is another world; that they

have immortal souls, and must give account of themselves to God, that they are exceeding sinful by nature and practice; that they are helpless in themselves; and confirms them in other things that are agreeable to some sound doctrine; the spirit that works thus operates as a spirit of truth; he represents things as they truly are.

[During the days of the JPM there were an abundance of counterfeits available and begging for attention. There were the Eastern religions—exotic, strange, alluring, sexy, far different from the religion of parents—a new and revolutionary paradigm altogether. Then there was magic, astrology, Satan worship, fortune telling, and much, much more; yet the Jesus People saw through those counterfeits fairly quickly and easily. Also, there were the political dimensions—the Vietnam War dispute, the civil rights movement—these had their allure as well. We marched in many anti-war protests, but we were handing out Christian literature that we had written and sometimes preaching at the rally points along the way. Some Jesus People would be pulled away and go astray, not so much by ideas as by the hormone-driven attractions of drugs, sex, and rock and roll, as we would say. It was usually temporary, followed by repentance and a renewed resolve.]

V. If the spirit that is at work among a people operates as a spirit of love to God and man, it is a sure sign that it is the Spirit of God.

Edwards' text, specifically 1 John 4:7-12, speaks of love to God and man, and thus it is plain that such love must be a characteristic of an awakening. His conclusion is that both were true of the awakening in New England.

> When the spirit that is at work amongst the people, tends this way, and brings many of them to high and exalting thoughts of the Divine Being, and his glorious perfections; and works in them an admiring, delightful sense of the excellency of Jesus Christ; representing him as the chief among ten thousand, and altogether lovely, and makes him precious to the soul; winning and drawing the heart with those motives and incitements to love, of which the apostle speaks in that passage of Scripture we are upon, viz. the wonderful, free love of God in giving his only-begotten Son to die for us, and the wonderful dying love of Christ to us, who had no love to him, but were his enemies; must needs be the Spirit of God.

Edward's observation was that when this love of God was evident it was also seen that,

> the spirit that quells contentions among men, and gives a spirit of peace and good will, excites to acts of outward kindness, and earnest desires of the salvation of souls—and causes a delight in those that appear as the children of God, and followers of Christ; I say, when a spirit operates after this manner among a people, there is the highest kind of evidence of the influence of a true and divine spirit.

However, Edwards knew that there was a counterfeit love that expressed itself in wild enthusiasm, a "kind of union and affection, arising from self-love." As might be expected, even a careful observer would have difficulty making a clear case for the counterfeit love Edwards speaks of. He knew of it but spent little time in explaining it. He does understand that the devil does not produce love of God and man.

> He will not give men a spirit of divine love, or Christian humility and poverty of spirit; nor could he if he would. He cannot give those things he has not himself; these things are as contrary as possible to his nature.

[The days of the JPM were marked by self-love and the erotic love of others—this was the spirit of the hippies. What counted was so-called freedom and the seeking of experiences of a decidedly fleshly nature, most often fueled by drugs.

What a difference God brought to those who were converted. Though many struggled and fell back into immature behavior, still the primary manifestation was an extraordinary love for God and other people. Yes, there were the counterfeits, as there always are—in, around, and often following an awakening. During even the height of the JPM was the Children of God, led by David Moses Berg, a group that twisted agape love into a love of the cult leader and a love of self in fulfilling bodily lusts. And there were other expressions of counterfeit love that I had to personally deal with in our own fellowship in San Francisco and Marin counties. As our little network of Christian houses expanded, much of my time was occupied in dealing with some of the aftermath of "love" gone wild. Still, the genuine was present, and when some of the old bunch gets together, we do vividly recall how it was that we experienced the love of God.

> **Having thus fulfilled what I at first proposed, in considering what are the certain, distinguishing marks..., whether it be the work of the Spirit of God or no; I now proceed to the APPLICATION.**

APPENDIX A

Section C
Practical Inferences.

I. From what has been said, I will venture to draw this inference, viz. That the extraordinary influence that has lately appeared, causing an uncommon concern and engagedness of mind about the things of religion, is undoubtedly, in the general, from the Spirit of God.

The awakening was evident in many places at once. It was "observed in a great multitude of people of all sorts, and in various places." Edwards concluded then that it could not be something contrived or put over as a "cheat."

> But when the work is spread over great parts of a country, in places distant from one another, among people of all sorts and of all ages, and in multitudes possessed of a sound mind, good understanding, and known integrity,... it is a sign of the influence of the Spirit of God.

"Uncommon appearances," were observed by Edwards and others. It would not have been overly unusual for there to be "crying out aloud, shrieking, being put into great agonies of body, &c." Edwards estimated these were of two sorts,

> ...either those who have been in great distress from an apprehension of their sin and misery; or those who have been overcome with a sweet sense of the greatness, wonderfulness, and excellency of divine things.

> Generally, in these agonies they have appeared to be in the perfect exercise of their

reason; and those of them who could speak, have been well able to give an account of the circumstances of their mind, and the cause of their distress, at the time, and were able to remember, and give an account of it afterwards. I have known a very few instances of those, who, in their great extremity, have for a short space been deprived, in some measure, of the use of reason; but among the many hundreds, and it may be thousands, that have lately been brought to such agonies, I never yet knew one lastingly deprived of their reason.

In addition to the emotions that would accompany the Holy Spirit's work of convicting of sin and then the joy that would come upon someone when they experienced God's saving grace, there were times that looked very much like what happened when demons would be cast out of people in the Gospel accounts, as in Mark 1:26 and Mark 9:26.

> Some have several turns of great agonies, before they are delivered; and others have been in such distress, which has passed off, and no deliverance at all has followed.

This particular section is long and complex and is not easily absorbed and understood. One last quote from Edwards and I leave this discussion:

> The imprudences and errors that have attended this work, are the less to be wondered at, if it be considered, that chiefly young persons have been the subjects of it, who have less steadiness and experience, and being in the

heat of youth, are much more ready to run to extremes.

[For Edwards, religion meant only Christianity. In the era of the JPM, Christianity was one among many religions that were coming to the fore. The surge of interest in Eastern religions, mainly Hinduism and Buddhism, neither Edwards nor I would attribute to the working of the Spirit of God. Whether that interest was to be expected in a youthful rebellion against authority, which was certainly a part of the hippie phenomenon, or was something more sinister in nature—an actual demonic counterfeit—is hard to know with any objective certainty. My own view is that there was a demonic nature to much of it, especially as various occult practices attached themselves to and eventually superseded in many ways the interest in Eastern religion. Therefore, the interest in spiritual things was not in itself a demonstration that the whole of the religious consciousness of that period was due to the Spirit of God.

As with the first awakening, the JPM suddenly appeared in many places at once, and most often with the same forms of ministry. Here I mean street evangelism, carried on mostly by persons in their twenties or younger and directed to persons of that same age grouping, tract and Bible distribution, Bible studies, small groups coming together to establish what we often called Christian houses, a focus on the person and work of Jesus Christ, boldly proclaiming Him as the only way to the Father, and so on. In my travels during the late 1960s this was readily apparent. I did not fully realize what I was seeing, but wherever I went, there it was, just exactly what I knew of in California's Bay Area.

As to "uncommon appearances"—this was minimal in the JPM, as far as my experience goes. There would be expressions of joy and thanksgiving but less public expression along the lines of what Edwards saw. As time went on, the JPM became more and more impacted by the Charismatic Movement, result-

ing in a shift in this area. This I observed in my travels. It would always bother me, and I would do what I could to maintain order and decorum. But this effort was not always successful, especially when uncommon behavior was supposedly done in "the name of the Lord."

Finally, the JPM was largely youth-oriented, and yes, some of what was observed could be attributed to youthful enthusiasm. As to the possibility that demons would be active in some and cause a lot of noise—this was a major part of my own experience in the JPM. In fact, I wrote two books about this during the 1970s. Not all of the Jesus People were engaged in the casting out of demons, but we were in San Francisco and Marin counties. This activity, which we called deliverance ministry, was a significant aspect of our ministry. The whole idea of Satan and demons was not something I embraced as a new believer; I only became convinced of it later on while living in the Anchor Rescue Mission in the Fillmore District of San Francisco during 1968. Though this might be unusual for someone in the Reformed Tradition, it nevertheless was something I experienced many hundreds of times and to which I hold now, though we see little of it in normal times.]

II. Let us all be hence warned, by no means to oppose, or do anything in the least to clog or hinder, the work; but, on the contrary, do our utmost to promote it. Now Christ is come down from heaven in a remarkable and wonderful work of his Spirit, it becomes all his professed disciples to acknowledge him, and give him honour.

The rejection of Jesus by the leaders of Israel during his earthly ministry is cited by Edwards as the chief example of opposing a work of God. The inference is that opposition to awakening in New England was tantamount to the same. This, in my thinking, is somewhat extreme on Edwards' part. And there are several other instances in the two final points of *Distinguishing marks* which, in my estimation, miss the mark.

Edwards, it is fairly apparent, adhered to a postmillennial view of the last days, in that Christ would establish his kingdom on earth and reign a thousand years before the predicted Second Advent. There was speculation that the awakening working among them might herald the beginning of that Messianic reign on earth. This, then, provided even more reason to support the awakening and especially not to oppose it. Edwards' position was,

> Whether the present work be the beginning of that great and frequently predicted coming of Christ to set up his kingdom, or not, it is evident, from what has been said, that it is a work of the same Spirit, and of the same nature.

There were reasons to oppose the awakening, and ministers like Boston's Charles Chauncy made them well known. Still, to tarnish the whole for weakness of a few parts was harmful. And Edwards warned,

> A work of God without stumbling-blocks is never to be expected. It must need be that offences come.

Edwards recognized the legitimacy of some of the opposition, especially the irregularities surrounding James Davenport and other extreme or unusual expressions of enthusiasm. He recognized that there must always be opposition to gospel work.

Edwards went father still—he suggested that opposition to the awakening might actually be a committing of the unpardonable sin.

> If there be any who still resolutely go on to speak contemptibly of these things, I would beg of them to take heed that they be not guilty of the unpardonable sin.

This does seem out of character for Edwards. But there it is.

The unpardonable sin, in my view and also in that of most people with a Reformed Theology, would be impossible for a genuinely born again Christian to commit. I assume that Edwards, as a convinced Calvinist, would adhere to the doctrine of the preservation or perseverance of the saints, so the idea that those who opposed the awakening would be in danger of committing the unpardonable sin, which is generally thought to be the attributing the working of the Holy Spirit to the devil, seems strange coming from Edwards' pen. (The unpardonable sin was committed against Jesus—his miracles were said to be generated by the prince of demons.) But there is an additional twist. Edwards suggested that it is not only active opposition he is referring to but passive opposition as well. This point, more than any of the others, may reveal a defensiveness on Edwards' part—which I do not find surprising, but is what I would expect from a man, however logical, faithful, and biblical, who had so much to defend and protect.

Edwards' next point is an appeal not only to refrain from opposing the awakening, but rather, to promote it. As a leader of the awakening and its strong supporter, this admonition came naturally to Edwards. It does seem, in examining the history of that awakening, that opposition both from within and without the awakening, did shorten or bring to a close in a general way the awakening, at least in New England and the middle colonies. Edwards saw this and it caused him some alarm.

[One of my regrets is my less than gracious attitude toward churches and pastors who criticized the JPM and my ministry in particular. On more than one occasion I ignored wise and godly

counsel from experienced Christian leaders, whom I unrighteously judged to be "not in the Spirit." And I was not alone in this. As an interest in charismatic gifts increased, those who did not so approve were consigned by those of us who were "filled with the Spirit" and "moving in the Spirit" to being "in the flesh" and even under the control of the devil.]

III. To apply myself to those who are the friends of this work, who have been partakers of it, and are zealous to promote it.

Edwards aimed to be not only a promoter but also a protector of the awakening. He knew what actions would be damaging, and he had ideas on how to prevent that damage:

> Let me earnestly exhort such to give diligent heed to themselves to avoid all errors and misconduct, and whatever may darken and obscure the work; and to give no occasion to those who stand ready to reproach it.

On this subject Edwards concludes his *Distinguishing Marks,* which is the longest of all his points. It is a fitting end to his concerns, because to participate in a moving of the Spirit of God can be dangerous to those who experience that moving. A sense of being better than, or more spiritual than, or more favored than others can easily assert itself. It is an issue of pride and will distort and defame the work.

> We had need, after such favours, in a special manner to keep a strict and jealous eye upon our own hearts, lest there should arise self-exalting reflections upon what we have received, and high thoughts of ourselves, as being now some of the most eminent of saints and pecu-

liar favourites of heaven, and that the secret of the Lord is especially with us.

He cautions then, "Let none think themselves out of danger of this spiritual pride."

Edwards acknowledged that some "true friends" of the awakening gave

> ...too much heed to impulses and strong impressions on their minds, as though they were immediate significations from heaven to them...

and then began to act on them. The result could have been the "imprudences and irregularities" much talked about by those who opposed the awakening. Some promoters of the awakening thought that God was restoring the "extraordinary gifts of the Spirit." Edwards did not agree and wished that such gifts would not be given. He made a distinction between times when there were extraordinary gifts given, as at the biblical Pentecost of Acts 2, and what have been called *normal* times, when the influences of the Spirit are "ordinary and gracious."

Iain Murray makes a similar distinction of normal verses awakening times. In the normal times, few are converted and the influences of the Spirit are ordinary, but in awakening times many are converted. Edwards believed the awakening was extraordinary but that there was an absence of extraordinary gifts. And this came before Pentecostalism made its appearance, by 166 years. He said,

> I do not expect a restoration of these miraculous gifts in the approaching glorious times of the church, nor do I desire it. It appears to me, that it would add nothing to the glory of those times, but rather diminish from it.

APPENDIX A

By the "glorious times" I think he means the anticipated establishing of Christ's kingdom on earth. His experience of the miraculous gifts was mixed at best, but he clearly did not favor them. For Edwards, the preaching of the gospel and the conversion of people to Christ was foremost—all else was a distraction from the real work. (Whether speaking in tongues was generally evident in the awakening is unknown. My estimation is that there were instances that some might call speaking in tongues, but Edwards did not directly speak of it.)

Edwards warned against judging the awakening and cites Jesus' advise to his disciples to refrain from pulling up the tares lest the good wheat be disturbed. Let judgment wait until the last great judgment day when God makes all things right and plain—this is his point. He especially counseled against judging whether a person is a Christian or not, behavior that both George Whitefield and George Tennent exhibited at points in their ministries. Additionally he cautioned that controversies with opposers not be conducted "with too much heat."

[These last sections of Edwards' Distinguishing Marks are the ones I needed most to understand during the JPM. This was an area where I was not always helpful to that working of God. I tended to be possessive and jealous. My error was masked as seeing myself as a guardian over the events that were taking place. I was quick to criticize and diminish. The primary areas of my concern were the tendency to wild enthusiasm, deviant theology, and sloppy Bible interpretation. At times, I think I hindered as much as I helped. I still do not know how to evaluate my role.

Those who knew me best thought I had the spiritual gift of discernment, which was much needed at the time. And there were indeed times when my opposition did prove of value. I did not think I was the only true minister of God, but at times I wondered why many pastors and churches had no part in the moving of the Spirit. Certainly, spiritual pride did take hold on some, most clearly on those who thought they were the first, the best, and the only ones who enjoyed God's special favor. What Edwards experienced in that first American awakening was also true of the JPM.

My view is that there were aspects of the first awakening that were probably not the result of the Spirit of God. It does not seem to me, despite his great effort to say otherwise, that Edwards thought that many of the affections, impressions, bodily movements, and so on, that he both personally observed or heard about, were from the Spirit. The same must be said for the JPM. But which is which is not so simple to determine. Over all, it is legitimate to say that the Spirit of God did mightily work in both these revivals. However, one must be cautious not to baptize the lot in the Holy Spirit. However sophisticated historians might become, weighing such factors as hysteria, mimicking, desiring to please preachers, approval of family and friends, and many other related issues, makes it difficult, if not impossible, to be dogmatic. Edwards' marks of a work of the Spirit of God are sufficient to persuade someone like me that there is a sovereign God who does pour out his Spirit when he wills.]

Appendix B:
Discussion and summary of Jonathan Edwards' The Religious Affections

The preface to Jonathan Edwards', *The Religious Affections,* is presented here followed by some thoughts I have on it. Then there is a simple listing of the "not certain signs" that Edwards felt were not genuine and Godly affections. Finally a listing of the "distinguishing signs" that Edwards felt were genuine and Godly affections. Jonathan Edwards, the careful analytic, wrote to the highest standards of his period, but to people like myself, his writing is difficult. Adding to that difficulty is the usage of terms that have changed over the course of a quarter of a millennium. I mean, Edwards is hard to understand.

Preliminary note: Jonathan Edwards began to see awakening in 1735. It is a good guess that the moving of God lasted until 1742, at least in the region where Edwards lived. His book, *The Religious Affections,* was written in 1746, and as Edwards evaluated what he saw at that time, his account is rather shocking.

Edwards' Introduction:

THERE is no question whatsoever, that is of greater importance to mankind, and what is more concerns every individual person to be well resolved in, than this: **What are the dis-**

tinguishing qualifications of those that are in favor with God, and entitled to his eternal rewards? Or, which comes to the same thing, **What is the nature of true religion? And wherein do lie the distinguishing notes of that virtue and holiness that is acceptable in the sight of God?** But though it be of such importance, and though we have clear and abundant light in the word of God to direct us in this matter, yet there is no one point, wherein professing Christians do more differ one from another. It would be endless to reckon up the variety of opinions in this point, that divide the Christian world; making manifest the truth of that declaration of our Savior, "Strait is the gate and narrow is the way, that leads to life, and few there be that find it."

The consideration of these things has long engaged me to attend to this matter, with the utmost diligence and care, and exactness of search and inquiry, that I have been capable of. It is a subject on which my mind has been peculiarly intent, ever since I first entered on the study of divinity. But as to the success of my inquiries it must be left to the judgment of the reader of the following treatise.

I am sensible it is much more difficult to judge impartially of that which is the subject of this discourse, in the midst of the dust and smoke of such a state of controversy, as this land is now in, about things of this nature. As it is more difficult to write impartially, so it is more difficult to read impartially. Many will probably be hurt in their spirits, to find so much that appertains to religious affection, here condemned: and perhaps indignation and contempt will be excited in others by finding so much here justified and approved. And it may be, some will be ready to charge me with inconsistency with myself, in so much approving some things, and so much condemning others; as I have found this has always been objected to by some, ever since the beginning of our late controversies about religion. It is a hard thing to be a hearty zealous friend of what has been good and glorious, in the late extraordinary appearances, and *to rejoice much in it; and at the same time to see the evil and pernicious tendency of what has been bad, and earnestly to oppose that. But yet, I am humbly but fully persuaded, we shall never be in the way of truth, nor go on in a way acceptable to God, and tending to the advancement of Christ's kingdom till we do so. There is indeed something very mysterious in it, that so much good, and so much bad, should be mixed together in the church of God; as it is a mysterious thing, and what has puzzled and amazed many a good Christian, that there should be that which is so divine and precious, as the saving grace of God, and the new and divine nature dwelling in the same heart, with so much corruption, hypocrisy, and iniquity, in a particular saint. Yet neither of these is more mysterious than real. And neither of them is a new or rare thing. It is no new thing, that much false religion should prevail, at a time of great reviving of true religion, and that at such a time multitudes of hypocrites should spring up among true saints. It was so in that great reformation, and revival of religion, that was in Josiah's time; as appears by Jeremiah 3:10, and 4:3, 4, and also by the great apostasy that there was in the land, so soon after his reign. So it was in that great outpouring of the Spirit upon the Jews, that was in the days of John the Baptist; as appears by the great apostasy of that people so soon after so general an awakening, and the temporary religious comforts and joys of many: John 5:35, "Ye were willing for a season to rejoice in his light." So it was in those great commotions that were among the multitude, occasioned by the preaching of Jesus Christ; of the many that were then called, but few were chosen; of the multitude that were roused and affected by his preaching, and at one time or other appeared mightily engaged, full of admiration of Christ, and elevated with joy, but few were true disciples, that stood the shock of the great trials that came afterwards, and endured to the end. Many were like the stony ground, or thorny ground; and but few, comparatively, like the good ground. Of the whole heap that was gathered, great part was chaff; that the wind afterwards drove away; and the heap of wheat that was left, was comparatively small; as appears abundantly, by the history of the New Testament. So it was in that great outpouring of the Spirit that was in the apostles' days as appears by Matthew 24:10-13. Galatians 3:1, and 4:11, 15. Philippians 2:21, and 3:18, 19, and the two epistles to the Corinthians, and many other parts of the New Testament. And so it was in the great reformation from Popery. It appears plainly to have been in the visible church of God, in times of great reviving of religion, from time to time, as it is with the fruit trees in the spring; there are a multitude of blossoms, all of which appear fair and beautiful, and there is a promising appearance of young fruits; but many of them are but of short continuance; they soon fall off, and never come to maturity.*

Not that it is to be supposed that it will always be so; for though there never will, in this world, be an entire purity, either in particular saints, in a perfect freedom from mixtures of corruption; or in the church of God, without any mixture of hypocrites with saints, and counterfeit religion, and false appearances of grace with true religion, and real holiness: yet it is evident, that there will come a time of much greater purity in the church of God, than has been in ages past; it is plain by these texts of Scripture, Isaiah 52:1. Ezekiel 44:6, 7, Joel 3:17. Zechariah 14:21. Psalm 69:32, 35, 36. Isaiah 35:8, 10, chap. 4:3, 4. Ezekiel 20:38. Psalm 37:9, 10, 21, 29. And one great reason of it will be that at that time God will give much greater light to his people, to distinguish between true religion and its counterfeits. Malachi 3:3, "And he shall sit as a refiner and purifier of silver: and he shall purify the sons of Levi, and purge them as gold and silver, that they may offer to the Lord an offering in righteousness." With ver. 18, which is a continuation of the prophecy of the same happy times. "Then shall ye return, and discern between the righteous and the wicked, between him that serveth God, and him that serveth him not."

It is by the mixture of counterfeit religion with true, not discerned and distinguished, that the devil has had his greatest advantage against the cause and kingdom of Christ, all along hitherto. It is by this means, principally, that he has prevailed against all revivings of religion, that ever have been since the first founding of the Christian church. By this, he hurt the cause of Christianity, in and after the apostolic age, much more than by all the persecutions of both Jews and Heathens. The apostles, in all their epistles, show themselves much more concerned at the former mischief, than the latter. By this, Satan prevailed against the reformation, began by Luther. Zwinglius, etc., to put a stop to its progress, and bring it into disgrace; ten times more, than by all those bloody, cruel, and before unheard of persecutions of the church of Rome. By this, principally, has he prevailed against revivals of religion, that have been in our nation since the reformation. By this he prevailed against New England, to quench the love and spoil the joy of her espousals, about a hundred years ago. And I think, I have had opportunity enough to see plainly that by this the devil has prevailed against the late great revival of religion in New England, so happy and promising in its beginning. Here, most evidently has been the main advantage Satan has had against us; by this he has foiled us. It is by this means, that the daughter of Zion in this land now lies on the ground, in such piteous circumstances as we now behold her; with her garments rent, her face disfigured, her nakedness exposed, her limbs broken, and weltering in the blood of her own wounds, and in no wise able to arise, and this, so quickly after her late great joys and hopes: Lamentations 1:17, "Zion spreadeth forth her hands, and there is none to comfort her: the Lord hath commanded concerning Jacob, that his adversaries shall be roundabout him: Jerusalem is as a menstruous woman among them." I have seen the devil prevail the same way, against two great revivings of religion in this country. Satan goes on with mankind, as he began with them. He prevailed against our first parents, and cast them out of *paradise, and suddenly brought all their happiness and glory to an end, by appearing to be a friend to their happy paradisaic state, and pretending to advance it to higher degrees. So the same cunning serpent, that beguiled Eve through his subtlety, by perverting us from the simplicity that is in Christ, hath suddenly prevailed to deprive us of that fair prospect, we had a little while ago, of a kind of paradisaic state of the church of God in New England.*

After religion has revived in the church of God, and enemies appear, people that are engaged to defend its cause, are commonly most exposed, where they are sensible of danger. While they are wholly intent upon the opposition that appears openly before them, to make head against that, and do neglect carefully to look all around them, the devil comes behind them, and gives a fatal stab unseen; and has opportunity to give a more home stroke, and wound the deeper, because he strikes at his leisure, and according to his pleasure, being obstructed by no guard or resistance.

And so it is ever likely to be in the church, whenever religion revives remarkably, till we have learned well to distinguish between true and false religion, between saving affections and experiences, and those manifold fair shows, and glistering appearances, by which they are counterfeited; the consequences of which, when they are not distinguished, are often inexpressibly dreadful. By this means, the devil gratifies himself, by bringing it to pass, that that should be offered to God, by multitudes, under a notion of a pleasing acceptable service to him, that is indeed above all things abominable to him. By this means he deceives great multitudes about the state of their souls; making them think they are something, when they are nothing; and so eternally undoes them; and not only so, but establishes many in a strong confidence of their eminent holiness, who are in God's sight some of the vilest of hypocrites. By this means, he many ways damps and wounds religion in the hearts of the saints, obscures and deforms it by corrupt mixtures, causes their religious affections woefully to degenerate, and sometimes, for a considerable time, to be like the manna that bred worms and stank; and dreadfully ensnares and confounds the minds of others of the saints and brings them into great difficulties and temptation, and entangles them in a wilderness, out of which they can by no means extricate themselves. By this means, Satan mightily encourages the hearts of open enemies of religion, and strengthens their hands, and fills them with weapons, and makes strong their fortresses; when, at the same time, religion and the church of God lie exposed to them, as a city without walls. By this means, he brings it to pass, that men work wickedness under a notion of doing God service, and so sin without restraint, yea with earnest forwardness and zeal, any with all their might. By this means he brings in even the friends of religion, insensibly to themselves, to do the work of enemies, by destroying religion in a far more effectual manner than open enemies can do, under a notion of advancing it. By this means the devil scatters the flock of Christ, and sets them one against another, and that with great heat of spirit, under a nation of zeal for God; and religion, by degrees degenerates into vain jangling; and during the strife, Satan leads both parties far out of the right way, driving each to great extremes, one on the right hand, and the other on the left, according as he finds they are most inclined, or most easily moved and swayed, till the right path in the middle is almost wholly neglected. And in the midst of this confusion, the devil has great opportunity to advance his own interest, and make it strong in ways innumerable, and get the government of all into his own hands and work his own will. And by what is seen of the terrible consequences of this counterfeit religion, when not distinguished from true religion, God's people in general have their minds unhinged and unsettled in things of religion, and know not where to set their foot, or what to think or do; and many are brought into doubts, whether there be anything in religion; and heresy, and infidelity, and atheism greatly prevail.

Therefore it greatly concerns us to use our utmost endeavors clearly to discern, and have it well settled and established, wherein true religion does consist. Till this be done, it may be expected, that great revivings of religion will be but of short continuance; till this be done, there is but little good to be expected of all our warm debates in conversation and from the press, not knowing clearly and distinctly what we ought to contend for.

My design is to contribute my mite, and use my best (however feeble) endeavors to this end, in the ensuing treatise; wherein it must be noted, that my design is somewhat diverse from the design of what I have formerly published, which was to show the distinguishing marks of a work of the Spirit of God, including both his common and saving operations; but what I aim at now, is to show the nature and signs of the gracious operations of God's Spirit, by which they are to be distinguished from all things whatsoever, that the minds of men are the subjects of, which are not of a saving nature. If I have succeeded, in this my aim, in any tolerable measure, I hope it will tend to promote the interest of religion. And whether I have succeeded to bring any light to this subject or no, and however my attempts may be reproached in these captious and censorious times, I hope in the mercy of a gracious God, for the acceptance of the sincerity of my endeavors; and hope also for the candor and prayers of the true followers of the meek and charitable Lamb of God.

A commentary on the Introduction

The very pastoral-minded Jonathan Edwards did not relish hurting people's feelings, but he felt a higher calling. He knew well that his book would be painful for many to read. This is evident when he said, "Many will probably be hurt in their spirits, to find so much that appertains to religious affection, here condemned: and perhaps indignation and contempt will be excited in others by finding so much here justified and approved." His sword would cut two ways; few would be happy with his conclusions.

"It is no new thing, that much false religion should prevail, at a time of great reviving of true religion, and that at such a time multitudes of hypocrites should spring up among true saints." Here is the mixture of the good and the bad. Edwards would not cover over the bad either, and he was aware, perhaps from conversations with his grandfather Solomon Stoddard, that outpourings of the Holy Spirit might come in the midst of an evil counterfeit, or, the other way around. He would say it was a mystery that it should be so and once said he does not attempt to reconcile the oddity. His interest is to provide a mechanism, however subjective, of distinguishing between the two extremes. He explains, "It is by the mixture of counterfeit religion with true, not discerned and distinguished, that the devil has had his greatest advantage against the cause and kingdom of Christ, all along hitherto."

One last quote, somewhat lengthy, that I heartily agree with:

> By this means the devil scatters the flock of Christ, and sets them one against another, and that with great heat of spirit, under a nation of zeal for God; and religion, by degrees degenerates into vain jangling; and during the strife, Satan leads both parties far out of the right way, driving each to great extremes, one on the right hand, and the other on the left, according as he finds they are most inclined, or most easily moved and swayed, till the right path in the middle is almost wholly neglected.

As I look back on the JPM I recognize that God did sovereignly act to save many out of a generation of youth that was headed to destruction in more ways than one. Over the years some of us who lived through that period and were impacted by it wonder at the magnitude of the dark sides of that awakening. And those dark side effects are yet in operation. It is indeed mysterious.

It is not surprising that Edwards found what he did, that an awakening could be accompanied by so much that was ungodly and evil. It has generally been the same in awakenings throughout history. Such it was with the Jesus People Movement. Without consulting my archives I can think of several aberrations that appeared in, around, and following the JPM. There was the Children of God founded by David Moses Berg and family. The Manifested Sons of God, a peculiar group, which along with the Children of God still exists, though under other names. The Shepherding Movement, long gone now but so successful in its time that it threatened to capture much of the JPM. Jim Jones and The People's Temple, now defunct, but not before eight hundred plus drank the poisonous Kool Aid punch.

Many have heard of the above groups and they have been the subject of some observation. Now, however, I will speak of something that I am only beginning to be aware of, or to be more exact, I am finally willing to admit.

Twice during my years as senior pastor of the Church of the Open Door in San Rafael, California, a church built by people converted during the JPM, I was admonished by mature and respected seminary professors.[54] Each warned me that whatever success my ministry might presently enjoy, the overall Christian community was not benefited.

I protested and defended. We had the Spirit. Sorry! Your churches had the Word but we had both Spirit and Word. Look at the numbers, the signs and wonders; we were the favored of God!

---

54 One a Baptist, the other a Presbyterian.

So it appeared to me and to those around me. I was not aware of the disunity I was sowing; I thought I was a champion of unity. A strange contradiction.

After all these years later I view things as did those two seminary professors. Not all, but many of the mini-denominations that emerged from the JPM days have served to foster competition and disunity. Imagine the following.

A new church rents a hall, replete with a musical band and a small army of young zealots. They beat the bushes and attract new people. Largely these are not new converts to Christ but people from nearby churches. These churches that have been "raided" would be evangelical churches. The Catholics, Presbyterians, Episcopalians, Lutherans, and other mainline and liturgical churches are not much impacted. It is a recycling of believers—no net growth. Am I being too harsh? I have found that pastors across the country would say amen to what I have just described.

Our Holy Ghost church raided local churches during the 1970s and I thought nothing of it. These new attendees were going where they were being fed—this was our rationale, or part of it. I am now embarrassed, and cannot help but think that I have, from time to time, received a certain kind of pay back—not fate or karma—but the fruit of what I had helped to plant.

My point is this: I resonate with what Edwards was saying in his preface. I would not put it in such stark terms of good versus evil, but maybe I ought to. Edwards was fearless, at least in his evaluation, not sparing anything or anyone, as there would be faces behind his "not certain signs" who would read his book. The issue is ultimate—heaven and hell and even more—the honor and glory of God.

I wonder how it would be, if the upstart groups joined with those who for many centuries have sought to advance the kingdom of God, rather than help produce a climate of competition and disunity. Probably these ideas are merely cluttering this page.

Summary of Edwards' book, *The Religious Affections* [55]

There will be no attempt to interpret or explain the signs either of those affections that Edwards did not consider to be clear evidence of true religion—"not certain signs"—or those he did—"distinguishing signs."

By "affections" I think Edwards meant the way a person was and lived his or her life in terms of actions, emotions, concerns, goals in life, and way of viewing God, others, and oneself. It might be said that the affections have to do with how love was acted out toward family, friends, the world, and most importantly, toward the Triune God.

Jonathan Edwards was a meticulous observer of human behavior, sometimes referred to as America's first psychologist, and his arguments are detailed, even pedantic in nature and scope. He was particularly concerned that he not be understood as a judge of all things spiritual and thus writes as to cover all issues.

"Not certain signs"

I. It is no sign one way or the other, that religious affections are very great, or raised very high.

II. It is no sign that affections have the nature of true religion, or that they have not, that they have great effects on the body.

III. It is no sign that affections are truly gracious affections, or that they are not, that they cause those who have them

---

55 The copy of *The Religious Affections* I use is published by Eremitical Press, Vancouver, 2009, ISBN-13 9781926777009.

to be fluent, fervent, and abundant, in talking of the things of religion.

IV. It is no sign that affections are gracious, or that they are otherwise, that persons did not make them themselves, or excite them of their own contrivance and by their own strength.

V. It is no sign that religious affections are truly holy and spiritual, or that they are not, that they come with texts of Scripture, remarkably brought to the mind.

VI. It is no evidence that religious affections are saving, or that they are otherwise, that there is an appearance of love in them.

VII. Persons having religious affections of many kinds, accompanying one another, is not sufficient to determine whether they have any gracious affections or no.

VIII. Nothing can certainly be determined concerning the nature of the affections, by this, that comforts and joys seem to follow awakenings and convictions of conscience, in a certain order.

IX. It is no certain sign that the religious affections which persons have are such as have in them the nature of true religion, or that they have not, that they dispose persons to spend much time in religion, and to be zealously engaged in the external duties of worship.

X. Nothing can be certainly known of the nature of religious affections by this, that they much dispose persons with their mouths to praise and glorify God.

XI. It is no sign that affections are right, or that they are wrong, that they make persons that have them exceeding confident that what they experience is divine, and that they are in a good estate.

XII. Nothing can be certainly concluded concerning the nature of religious affections, that any are the subjects of, from this, that the outward manifestations of them, and the relation persons give of them, are very affecting and pleasing to the truly godly, and such as greatly gain their charity, and win their hearts.

Distinguishing signs

I. Affections that are truly spiritual and gracious, do arise from those influences and operations on the heart, which are spiritual, supernatural and divine.

II. The first objective ground of gracious affections, is the transcendently excellent and amiable nature of divine things as they are themselves; and not any conceived relation they bear to self, or self-interest.

III. Those affections that are truly holy, are primarily founded on the loveliness of the moral excellency of divine things. Or, (to express it otherwise) a love of divine things for the beauty and sweetness of their moral excellency is the first beginning and spring of all holy affections.

IV. Gracious affections do arise from the mind's being enlightened, richly and spiritually to understand or apprehend divine things.

V. Truly gracious affections are attended with a reasonable and spiritual conviction of the judgment, of the reality and certainty of divine things.

VI. Gracious affections are attended with evangelical humiliation. Evangelical humiliation is a sense that a Christian has of his own utter insufficiency, despicableness, and odiousness, with an answerable frame of heart.

VII. Another thing, wherein gracious affections are distinguished from others, is, that they are attended with a change of nature.

VIII. Truly gracious affections differ from those affections that are false and delusive, in that they tend to, and are attended with the lamblike, dovelike spirit and temper of Jesus Christ; or in other words, they naturally beget and promote such a spirit of love, meekness, quietness, forgiveness and mercy, as appears in Christ.

IX. Gracious affections soften the heart, and are attended and followed with a Christian tenderness of spirit.

X. Another thing wherein those affections that are truly gracious and holy, differ from those that are false, is beautiful symmetry and proportion.

XI. Another great and very distinguishing difference between gracious affections and others is, that gracious affections, the higher they are raised, the more is a spiritual appetite and longing of soul after spiritual attainments increased. On the contrary, false affections rest satisfied in themselves.

XII. Gracious and holy affections have their exercise and fruit in Christian practice. I mean, they have that influence and power upon him who is the subject of them, that they cause that a practice, which is universally conformed to, and directed by Christian rules, should be the practice and business of his life.

Appendix C:
Movements that preceded and followed the Jesus People Movement

What follows is, one, a brief and undocumented account of what may have influenced or impacted the Jesus People Movement, and two, a short discussion of three movements that may or may not be connected to or somehow associated with the JPM.

One—that which preceded

The JPM certainly did not originate in a vacuum. How and by what it was influenced is not clear to me. However, with that acknowledged, there are events that are sometimes credited as having impacted the JPM.

The Wesleyan Holiness Movement

Sometime after the death of the great Methodist, John Wesley, his followers, who were encouraged by Wesley's view of sanctification, developed a theology focused on holiness. One of the variations on this theme posited that one could live a holy life utterly without sinning, made possible through a second working or baptism of the Holy Spirit. Over the course of time doubt was cast upon this view, and it occasionally proved difficult, even embarrassing, for those who had embraced it. Though some Christians continue to hold to the doctrine with modifications, it is probable that early Pentecostalism emerged from the Wesleyan holiness movement.

The Azusa Street Revival

Modern Pentecostalism was born in 1906 at a meeting house on Azusa Street in Los Angeles, California, and some of its early leaders had been involved in the Wesleyan holiness movement. Instead of holiness, they considered that tongue-speaking was the evidence of true conversion, a gift that resulted from the baptism (or second blessing) of the Holy Spirit. (The first baptism or first blessing of the Holy Spirit would be the new birth.) It is probable that the charismatic movement, which appeared more than half a century later, owed its existence to Azusa Street, though the 1960s' emphasis on the gifts of the Holy Spirit did not always share the same theology as early Pentecostalism.

The Healing Revival of the 1950s

At the Odd Fellows Hall on Dekum Street between 6th and 7th avenues in Northeast Portland, Oregon, two blocks from where I lived from 1944 to 1955, wild Pentecostal healing meetings caught the attention of the neighborhood. A bunch of us kids would sneak in just to watch the fun. My parents would talk of it (this was before my dad's conversion), and they laughed about the "holy rollers."

It was not until much later in my life, after talking with some of the kids with whom I had gone to Woodlawn Elementary School that I learned of the nature of those meetings at the Odd Fellows Hall. It was part of the Healing Revival that swept through the country and attracted, for the most part, second generation Pentecostals.

It was William Marrion Branham (1909-1965) who is often credited with founding the faith healing movement shortly after World War II. Up until his death he popularized healing among Pentecostals. Many of his supporters considered him more than a healer, however, and he became known as a healer-prophet. Some even expected him to return from the dead. It was said that an angel aided him in his ministry. Branham's success and notoriety resulted in others following in his footsteps. Virtually the same format he developed is in use to this day among the faith healers.

It may be that the healing revival of the 1950s did influence the JPM. I myself was caught up in the phenomenon and witnessed some dramatic healings during the JPM. Whether these healing events were a direct result of the outpouring of signs and wonders that did occur during the JPM and which faded after the JPM subsided, or whether they filtered down to us from the 1950s, is something I cannot authoritatively answer. If pressed, I would say that the miracles of healing we saw during the JPM owed themselves only to the power of a sovereign God, because they were unusual and not normal. The healings started and then ended; it was not a matter of our theology or methodology.

The Catholic Renewal and Charismatic Movements

The JPM was definitely impacted by the charismatic movement, which had itself been impacted by twentieth century Pentecostalism. And to complicate matters, there was also the Catholic Renewal movement, which had its own associated charismatic elements.

As I stated in the body of the book, I am not sure of what influenced what or what came first or followed, but all of these movements touched the JPM in some manner. It may be many years or even generations from now before the dynamics will all be unraveled. If pressed, I would say that the JPM was separate and apart from any prior movement but intersected, to varying degrees, with Pentecostalism, Catholic Renewal, and the charismatic movement—at least by 1970. What I mean is that at around 1970 I noticed a marked change. From 1967 to 1970 the emphasis was on mission and evangelism.

As the 1970s progressed, charismatic gifts seemed to be the primary focus, and by that I mean speaking in tongues, healing, and prophecy.

Impact of pentecostal understandings on evangelism

As a charismatic/pentecostal (I use this awkward phrase, because I was often unsure of exactly how to identify myself) I held to general Arminian views of conversion. By that I mean I wanted to have someone pray the sinner's prayer in order to receive Jesus as Savior and Lord. My favorite tool was the *Four Spiritual Laws*, published by Campus Crusade for Christ. It was a rare event that when the end of the tiny booklet was reached, a person did not go ahead and pray the prayer. Grounded now in a Reformed theology, I do not do this, because I expect the Holy Spirit of God to bring conversion after a presentation of the law and grace gospel. But, my point here is that with a charismatic/pentecostal-influenced Arminianism, the goal was to get someone speaking in tongues. The thinking was that no one could speak in tongues without the indwelling power and presence of the Holy Spirit.

At first I struggled with this. It seemed wrong to merely work to get people speaking in tongues without some kind of telling of the gospel. Early on I often combined the two. Later, instead of using the tracts or the "Roman Road," we simply relied on our praise and worship team, of which I was a part. We played the choruses that we learned would easily move into what we called "singing in the Spirit." Such singing was a musical form of speaking in tongues, or so we thought. It was not difficult to get everyone singing and swaying, eyes closed, arms lifted, and the mellow sound of hundreds of voices speaking in or singing in tongues. Once we heard that noise we assumed conversion had been accomplished. Now the tools used were a bass, lead, and rhythm guitar, all playing to the beat of the drum. Sometimes the work would come quickly, other times it might take an hour or so. After a while, I am now embarrassed to say, I became very skilled at this practice.

A sharp contrast

Before moving on to the next section there is one contrast between the Jesus Movement and the general charismatic and Pentecostal influences that I would like to express. It has to do with the gift of prophecy.

Though I am now, since 1995, in the process of moving toward a Reformed theology, I am not a cessationist. Generally cessationism is the view that the gifts of the Holy Spirit—mainly the "power gifts" like healing, speaking in tongues, and prophecy—ceased with the publication of the New Testament. It is more nuanced than that, but the above definition describes the position.

There were a number of times when I heard people make statements that were prophetic in nature, in that something in the future was predicted. Such came not always in meetings that featured a lot of music of any kind or in long drawn out prayer meetings. It was in more ordinary, matter-of-fact kind of circumstances, and no one made a big deal of it. There were several times when I spoke things that had just come to me that proved to be exactly spot on. At the time I did not know whether to describe what I experienced as a word of knowledge, as found in 1 Corinthians 12:8, or as prophecy. On two occasions, what I seemed to be told by God was nothing short of amazing and had the effect of bringing him glory. In nearly every single event where I had either a word of knowledge or a prophecy I was alone. For a number of years I witnessed these events and began to think it was all quite regular and normal.

This changed, however, after we learned better how to do things from the charismatic/pentecostal preachers and teachers to whose gatherings we began to flock. This was near the ending of the JPM however. Then the "power gifts" would be exercised in meetings featuring a lot of music, praise, prayer, and getting in touch with or experiencing the Spirit, or so we thought.

It is likely that gifts of the Holy Spirit may be evident in times of genuine awakenings, or not; it is not a cookie cutter situation. It is probable at minimum, and I think highly likely, that people will manufacture or replicate, however innocently, what they see others are doing. By the time of the JPM there were many well-known faith healers and people who "moved in the spirit" that we learned from. What we saw we mimicked and imitated. We wanted to be like them; they had tapes and books for sale, and were well-respected amongst Pentecostals and charismatics. And we baptized it all in the Spirit—our guards were down since we did not have the maturity to cope with conflict and express disapproval or dissent. What we took to be authentic expressions of Holy Spirit ministry was, from my present vantage point, something far different. And it is such humanly engineered pseudo-spirituality that is truly the dark side of revival.

Two—that which followed[56]

Not understanding that awakenings come and go at the will of a sovereign God, many of us who were active in the JPM wanted this extraordinary out-working of the power of God to continue. And desiring things we did not understand may have contributed to our attributing to God that which was the ordinary and normal working and planning by humans, which may be successful—to a degree.

The Vineyard and John Wimber (Third Wave)

The JPM dramatically changed, at least in California, once Chuck Smith's Calvary Chapel and other groups, including the

---

[56] There will be some overlap here with material found in the chapter 4 on the Jesus People Movement. This is intentional as I thought it might be helpful to have this appendix be a stand-alone essay.

churches of the Open Door that I was part of, were up and running. [57]

There was almost a *spiritual* explosion that followed the involvement of Lonnie Frisbee with Calvary Chapel in Costa Mesa.[58] Then in 1970 John Wimber emerged out of Calvary Chapel, and the Vineyard was born, and with it an emphasis on church growth. It was in Pasadena at Fuller Theological Seminary that I first encountered John Wimber as he taught at the church growth seminars during the mid-1980s. The term "Third Wave" has been used to describe what was taking place as a result of the emphasis on church growth, and it did influence me in Mill Valley—for a while anyway.

Mega churches soon came on the scene, and there were thousands of new church starts; evangelical Christianity was on the move, and some thought the Jesus People Movement was still alive.

The church growth movement might have been an extension of or a continuation of the JPM, but I do not think so. The awakening that was the JPM was over, and the emphasis on church growth was actually necessitated by the large numbers of new believers who needed spiritual homes. By 1980 the last vestiges of the JPM had vanished from the San Francisco Bay Area and other places I traveled—despite what was going on in the Los Angeles area. The new emphasis was not the preaching of the gospel or teaching of the Bible, but it was

---

57 I consider my views to be part of the "intramural" debate among Christians. I would not engage is such a discussion if I had not been personally involved and thus implicated. There is a way in which this appendix is a form of therapy for me personally. I can speak to issues, because I am also critiquing myself.

58 Lonnie and I spent many hours together walking the streets of the Haight-Ashbury and hanging out at the Living room run by Ted Wise, Danny Sands, Rick Zacks, and others. Lonnie lived at the House of Acts in Novato, where I spent a considerable amount of time in fellowship with my friends. After Lonnie moved back home to Costa Mesa he phoned me and asked me to bring some of the brothers with me and help evaluate whether he should involve himself with some Christians he had met. David Hoyt, Danny Sands, Rick Zacks, and I drove down and spent several hours talking with Chuck Smith and a number of his elders or deacons. Our view was that it would be good for Lonnie and the fledgling ministry that was developing to be in partnership with the church that Chuck Smith was pastoring.

growth for growth's sake, with entertainment-centered social bonding processes and the meeting of felt needs stoking the new movement. Perhaps my evaluation is harsh, but this was what I thought then and continue to think now.

The Toronto Blessing

Out of the Vineyard and Calvary Chapel church planting efforts, along with dozens of other smaller groups also reaching out, was born in Toronto, Canada, a phenomenon which became known as the Laughing Revival, or the Toronto Blessing, or the River, etc. (There was also a similar, but distinct revival excitement reported at Brownsville, Florida; I think they were really twin movements.) I followed these closely and hoped to see signs of the Spirit in them. As time went on, connections between some of the dark sides of the first and second awakenings, the excesses and aberrations, began to be reported by a number of sources. It then appeared, to me anyway, that what was hoped to be a genuine working of the Spirit of God was merely human-engineered dynamics accompanied with attempts to recapture the excitement of the JPM. As a result of various essays that I have written about the Toronto Blessing, which can be found at www.earthenvesseljournal.com, I have been accused several times of committing the sin of the blasphemy of the Holy Spirit—so sure some were that it was all a genuine working of the Spirit.

On a number of occasions I had the opportunity to visit meetings where some of those who were supposed to have the "anointing" were speaking, mostly at Bethel Church in Redding, California, but what I experienced was anything but a time when God convicted of sin and revealed Jesus as Savior through the preaching of a biblical gospel. More often than not I was disappointed, sometimes even angered.

To me, the revivals, whether of human or divine origin, stemming from the Airport Vineyard Church in Toronto, bore no resemblance to the JPM.

The "Fourth Wave"?

There are some who contest that there is now a "fourth wave" of the Spirit. The first wave would be the early 1900s pentecostal movement begun at Azusa Street in Los Angeles, the second would be the 1950s healing revival coupled with the Catholic Renewal and Charismatic Movements, with the JPM tacked on as part of these, the third would be the work of John Wimber and the Vineyard, coupled now with the ministry of Bill Johnson of Bethel Church in Redding, California and the so-called, Kansas City Prophets, among whom are Bob Jones, Paul Cain, and Mike Bickle. Also, connected or somehow associated with these are MorningStar Publications and Ministries founded by Rick Joyner in Fort Mill, South Carolina. Whether this is the third or fourth wave depends on who you are talking to. But the fourth wave is supposedly going on now in this early part of the twenty-first century and evidenced by such people as Benny Hinn, Joel Olsteen plus those who are identified with the so-called third wave , Bob Jones and the other Kansas City Prophets, along with Bill Johnson of Bethel Church and Rick Joyner of MorningStar. Some, however, contest that the fourth wave began with the Toronto Blessing. However it may be, and it would all be mere speculation, I can only say that I doubt there is any connection, least of all a continuation, of the JPM in anything observers have labeled the third or fourth wave.

The emphasis on that which is denoted the third or fourth wave is very much the same as the first and second wave. Each has an emphasis on health and wealth, and, though proponents of the waves would object to my analysis, there is very little mention of the Gospel of Christ. Due to such criticism promoters of the "waves" go out of their way to make some mention of the time-honored biblical emphases; however, their focus is still healings, prophecies, and other "spiritual" phenomenon. More important is the new things that God is revealing through the restoration of the so-called "five-fold ministry." Biblical references, if any, are merely tacked on in order to lend credence to the new revelations from the anointed leaders.

The JPM was centered on the new birth and Bible-based teachings—at least in the early years from 1967 to 1970. As the Pentecostal/charismatic teachings impacted the JPM, the original focus was altered.

An explanation

Those religious movements that preceded the JPM did influence it in ways that are at present uncertain. Influence is one thing, but such would not mean continuation or initiation. The JPM stands alone as something that began and ended, as do all genuine awakenings produced by the Holy Spirit of God, despite what went before—and the whole of the history of the Christian Church went before and in every way shaped the JPM.

As to what followed the JPM—it is characteristic of awakenings that they begin and end. Yes, the second awakening was long in duration, beginning in about 1798 and ending in about 1825 or 1835 depending on how the ministry of Charles Finney is considered, but the form and shape of all that has recently excited certain segments of the Christian Church is very different from that which was the JPM.

There is yet another view

When Arthur Conan Doyle's Sherlock Holmes was summoned to a crime scene he would examine the evidence and then develop a theory that accounted for all the evidence at hand, and that theory must be correct, even if it seemed incredible or preposterous to others. The following may be a Holmesean type theory:

Since the Azusa Street Revival, Pentecostalism has very powerfully influenced American evangelism, almost to the point of usurping it. Evidence of this is seen in the early revival itself, then the Aimee Semple McPherson phenomenon, followed by William Branham and the healing revival, then the Catholic Renewal. At almost the same time came the Charismatic Movement and the combination of all of this was the growth of the charismatic denominations like Calvary Chapel, The Vineyard, and multiple other small denominations emerging from the church growth movement. And now something which is being referred to as the fourth wave, and is being seen all around the world is, in my opinion, a replacement of traditional Protestant Christianity with what might be called "Pentecostalisms"

Right in the middle of it all, however, was a genuine work of the Spirit of God called the Jesus People Movement. And this Jesus People Movement was hijacked, to some degree, by what went before and has been distorted, as far as its true identity, by that which followed. Does this theory square with the evidence?

Index

a Kempis, Thomas, 113
Adventist(s), 55, 56, 57, 64, 79
Allen, Ethan, 37
Anchor Rescue Mission, 86, 100, 158
Arminian (-ist, -ism), 42, 48, 52-3, 56, 60, 73, 112, 124, 183
Asbury, Francis, 46, 53
Azusa Street Revival, 181, 188, 189
Babson, Roger, 65
Baptists, 8, 26, 28, 32, 36, 39, 40, 41, 42, 56, 57, 58, 59, 63, 64, 75, 79, 86, 92, 100
Barnes, Gilbert H., 58
Basham, Don, 78, 107
Baxter, Ern, 78, 107
Beardsley, Frank, 8, 9, 34, 46, 50, 55, 57, 116-17, 120
Beecher, Henry Ward, 68, 111
Beecher, Lyman, 44, 45
Berg, David, 90-1, 103-04, 105, 106, 143, 154, 174
Bethel Church in Redding, 187, 188
Bhaktivendanta, Swami, 83
Bickle, Mike, 188
Blair, Samuel, xvii, 18, 60
Branham, William Marrion, 181-82, 190
Brownsville Revival, 51, 187
Buckley, Mark, 93, 94
Burr, Aaron, 21, 27
Caen, C. C., 8-9, 119
Cain, Paul, 188

Calvary Chapel, 96, 185, 186, 187, 190
Calvin, John, 113
Calvin(-ism, -ist), 17, 19, 30, 42, 44, 45, 46, 47, 50, 52, 53, 60, 73, 112, 124, 140, 160
camp meetings, 29, 39-41, 49, 50, 63, 65, 68
Campus Crusade for Christ, 183
Cane Ridge, 40, 50. See also camp meetings
Cartwright, Peter, 41-42, 63, 74, 111
Catholic(s), 175
Catholic Renewal, 76, 77, 78, 79, 136, 182-83, 188, 190
cessation (-ism, -ist), 184
Chambers, Talbot W., 64
charismatic, 23, 70, 79, 80, 95, 100, 104, 105, 106, 115, 136, 138, 161, 183, 184, 185, 189, 190
Charismatic Movement, 72, 76, 77, 78, 79, 99, 136, 149, 157, 181, 182-83, 188, 190
Chauncy, Charles, 28, 29-30, 141, 159
Children of God (COG), 90, 103-05, 106, 107, 133, 143, 154, 174
Christian Houses, xiii, xiv, 82, 86, 87-9, 90, 91, 92, 93, 98, 99, 100, 108, 110, 115, 154, 157, 186
Christian Science, 55, 57, 79
Christian World Liberation Front, 98
Civil War, 61, 74, 75, 111
Cleveland, Catherine C., 51, 52, 54

Coke, Thomas, 53
Congregational, (-ist), 14, 19, 28, 32, 36, 37, 39, 44, 48, 58, 59, 130
Darby, John Nelson, 56
Davenport, James, 26, 27-30, 141, 143, 159
Davies, Samuel, xvii, 60, 62, 111, 149
Day, Howard, 86
deliverance ministry, 102, 109, 135, 147, 158
Dickinson, Jonathan, xvii, 24, 60, 62, 111
DuBose, Dr. Francis, 81-82, 86, 87
Dwight, Timothy, 42-44, 46, 58, 60, 63, 111
Eddy, Mary Baker, 57
Edwards, Jonathan, xvii, 1, 8, 16, 17, 18, 19-21, 23, 24, 25, 26, 29, 30, 31, 36, 37, 42, 43, 44, 49, 60, 62, 74, 111, 117, 118, 119-120, 130-64, 165-79
Edwards, Timothy, 19
Emerging Church Movement, 109
Episcopal, (-ian), 32, 59, 78, 175
Eskridge, Larry, xiv-xv, xx, 76
Ewald, Father Todd, 78
Finley, Samuel, 18
Finney, Charles G., xvii, 36, 37, 44, 45-49, 58, 60, 63, 65, 66, 72, 74, 111, 113, 121, 189
Fourth Wave, 188, 190
Frampton, Kenneth, 105
Franklin, Benjamin, 22
Frelinghuysen, Theodore, 16-17, 18, 62
Frisbee, Lonnie, 86, 90, 103, 186
Gale, George W., 46
Gasper River, 40. *See also* camp meetings
General Camp Meetings, 39. *See also* camp meetings
Girard, Chuck, 96

Golden Gate Baptist Theological Seminary, xiv, 81, 82, 83, 86, 87, 93, 99
Gossett, Al, 87, 88
Graham, Billy, 113
Griffin, Edward Dorr, 36, 44
Half-way Covenant, 15, 16, 21, 130
Hare Krishna temple, 83, 106
healing(s), 4, 5, 72, 76, 77, 78, 80, 89, 99, 100, 101, 102, 103, 107, 109, 136, 138, 181-82, 183, 184, 185, 188, 190
Hinn, Benny, 188
His Place, 98
Hooker, Thomas, 18
Hopkins, Kenny, 94, 95
House Ministries, 89. *See also* Christian Houses
House of Miracles, 90. *See also* Christian Houses
Hoyt, David, xvii, xviii, 83, 87, 89, 90, 91, 98, 103, 104, 143, 186
Hyde, Alvin, 36
Jefferson, Thomas, 21, 37
Jehovah's Witnesses, 55, 56, 57, 79
Jews, Jewish, 73-74, 86, 99, 124, 128, 134, 167, 169
Johnson, Bill, 188
Jones, Bob, 188
Jones, Jim, 105-07, 143, 144, 174
Joyful Noise, 93-96, 98
Joyner, Rick, 188
Kansas City Prophets, 188
Kidd, Thomas S., xx, 10, 27, 34-35
Kuhlman, Kathryn, 78
Lamphier, Jeremiah, 66, 67, 111
Lattin, Don, 103
Laughing Revival, 51, 133, 187
Lewis, C. S., 113
Lewis, Pastor Bob, 80-81
Lincoln, Abraham, 42
Lincoln Park Baptist Church, 82, 87, 88, 100

INDEX

Lindsay, Hal, 99
Living Room, The, 86, 90, 186
Log College, 18, 23
Luther, Martin, xix, 113, 169
Lutheran(s), 17, 175
Manning, Dr. Jack, 99
Maranatha, 96
McGee, John, 40
McGee, William, 39
McGready, James, 39-40, 63, 74
Methodist(s), 22, 26, 36, 39, 40, 41, 42, 46, 53, 58, 59, 63, 75, 82, 180
Miller, William, 56, 57, 64
Mills, Samuel J., 59
miracle(s), xviii, 4, 5, 47, 88, 89, 91, 100, 107, 110, 122, 143, 144, 160, 182. *See also* signs and wonders.
Mormon(s), (-ism), 52, 55, 56, 64, 79
MorningStar Pub. & Min., 188
Mueller, George, 92, 93
Mumford, Bob, 78, 107, 108
Murray, Andrew, 113
Murray, Iain H., xx, 8, 9, 22, 38, 40, 45, 48, 52, 53, 112-16, 120, 162
Nee, Watchman, 113
Nettleton, Asahel, xvii, 44-45, 46, 47, 48, 60, 63, 74, 111
New Lights, 18, 54, 146
Old Lights, 18, 23, 24, 26, 28, 139, 141
Olsteen, Joel, 188
One Way theology, xiii, 6, 98, 118
Orr, J. Edwin, xx, 36, 57, 61, 62, 64, 65, 68, 71, 72, 73
Paine, Thomas, 37
Palmer, Phoebe, 61, 65, 67, 111
Payson, Edward, 44
Pentecostal, (-ism), 4, 50, 60, 70, 72, 78, 79, 99, 100, 106, 115, 138, 162, 181, 182, 183, 184, 185, 188, 189, 190
People's Temple, 105-07, 143, 174. *See also* Jones, Jim

Pietism, 17
Plowman, Ed, 86
Presbyterian(s), 18, 19, 32, 36, 39, 40, 41, 46, 58, 63, 174, 175
Prince, Derek, 78, 107
Princeton University, 18, 21, 24, 46
prophet(s), (-ic), 52, 64, 101, 126, 132, 136, 137, 149, 182, 184, 188
Puritan(s), 19, 25, 28, 44
Quaker(s), 32
Reformed theology, xix, 5, 42, 45, 47, 48, 50, 60, 64, 66, 124, 125, 128, 146, 158, 160, 183, 184
River, The, 51, 133, 187
Roberts, Oral, 78
Robinson, William, 18
Rosen, Moishe (Martin), 86, 99
Rowland, John, 18
Russell, Charles Taze, 56, 57
San Quentin Prison, 94, 108
Shepherding Movement, 107-08, 143, 174
Simpson, Charles, 78, 107
signs and wonders, xiv, 4-6, 72, 99, 100, 101-03, 106, 107, 108, 144, 174, 182. *See also* miracles
slave(s), (-ry), 42, 58-59, 68, 75
Smith, Chuck, 90, 185, 186
Smith, Joseph, 52, 56, 64
Soul Inn, 82, 88, 89, 100, 110. *See also* Christian Houses
Spring, Gardiner, 44
Spurgeon, C. H., 22, 113
Stoddard, Solomon, 1, 8, 14-16, 17, 18, 19, 37, 38, 42, 43, 130, 173
Stone, Barton, 39, 40, 54, 63, 111
Streeter, John, 86
Sweeney, Ed, 104
Tennent, Gilbert, John, William, xvii, 18, 21, 23, 24, 25, 26, 27, 29, 49, 60, 62, 111, 141, 149, 163
Third Wave, 185-86, 188

Toronto Blessing, 51, 115, 133, 187, 188
Torrey, R. A., 113
Unitarianism, 37
Vineyard, The, 185, 186, 187, 188, 190
Weeks, William R., 45
Wesley, Charles, 22
Wesley, John, 20, 22, 48, 49, 111, 113, 180
Wesleyan Holiness Movement, 180, 181
Whitefield, George, xvii, 17, 18, 20, 21, 22-25, 27, 29, 31, 32, 34, 36, 47, 49, 60, 62, 74, 111, 134, 141, 149, 163
Wimber, John, 185, 186, 188
Wise, Ted, 86, 90, 186
Yale University (College), 19, 42, 43, 58, 63
Zion's Inn, 87, 89, 91

Other Books by Kent Philpott

For Pastors of Small Churches

How to Care for Your Pastor

Are You Really Born Again? Understanding True and False Conversion

Are You Being Duped?

Why I Am a Christian

How Christians Cast Out Demons Today

ALSO AVAILABLE THROUGH OUR WEBSITE IS:

From Death into Life by William Haslam

For ordering please go to: http://www.earthenvessel.net

CPSIA information can be obtained
at www.ICGtesting.com
Printed in the USA
JSHW010843300423
40939JS00003B/149